CHOOSING
to be
CATHOLIC

FOR THE FIRST TIME, OR ONCE AGAIN

CHOOSING *to be* CATHOLIC

FOR THE FIRST TIME, OR ONCE AGAIN

WILLIAM J. O'MALLEY, S.J.

ThomasMore®
~*Bringing Faith to Life*~

Allen, Texas

Send all inquiries to:
Thomas More® Publishing
200 East Bethany Drive
Allen, Texas 75002-3804

Telephone: 877-275-4725 / 972-390-6300
Fax: 800-688-8356 / 972-390-6560

Visit us at: **www.thomasmore.com**

Customer Service E-mail: **cservice@rcl-enterprises.com**

Printed in the United States of America

Library of Congress Control Number: 2001092426

ISBN: 0-88347-473-5

2 3 4 5   05 04 03 02

FOR GERALD BLASZCZAK, S.J.
AND ROBERT SEALY, S.J.

CONTENTS

I believe. Help my unbelief!
—Mark 9:25

INTRODUCTION

In his Pulitzer Prize-winning stories, collected in book form as *Parish!*, Robert F. Keeler describes a young woman about to commit herself to study for the Rite of Christian Initiation of Adults. "In the autumn twilight, Audrey Scheneman steered her car into the parish parking lot, turned off the ignition and began to struggle with powerfully opposing impulses." Her father was Jewish, her mother was Catholic, but they had raised her in neither religion. But after a very serious accident, she began attending Mass with her boyfriend, Nick Viscardi. Out of the blue, she received an invitation to an introductory meeting for RCIA (not realizing her boyfriend had submitted her name). "But as she began to leave her car that first night, second thoughts overwhelmed her. 'I never had a really great comfort level with clergy,' she said. 'I was terrified.' On the third try, she persuaded herself to cross the street and go to the meeting, upstairs in the parish center. . . . A few minutes later, it was her turn to introduce herself to the others. 'I thought I was going to pass out,' she said."

This book is for Audrey and all the hesitant and good hearts like her, who feel they just might be missing something—and not really quite sure they want to find out what it is. For most of us, any strange group is off-putting, and religion is one of those subjects that . . . "Well, we just don't talk about those things." Even worse, they'll bring up all kinds of mysterious stuff that only theologians care about, when all we want is just a sense of wholeness and peace.

But this book is also for those who, for many reasons, became disenchanted with the Church or perhaps even with God himself. The liturgy didn't speak to their spiritual needs; the "rules" seemed somehow unreasonable; those church folk from whom they sought advice or consolation came up lacking; God seemed to betray their trust in him. For whatever reasons, they "drifted away" from religious practice, even though, when asked "Religion?" on forms, they still automatically wrote "Catholic." At some point later in their lives—again for unaccountable reasons—they felt a kind of formless need within themselves for something more meaningful than merely surviving the workaday world, a kind of "context" or background in which they could find reasons for going on, for preserving integrity in a world which seems to have foresworn it, connection to an energizing "Presence" who is an assurance that, no matter what, they are not alone. They are looking for a dimension to their lives that can come only from discovering again the sense of being "at home" which they had when religion was still a meaningful part of their lives, a dimension that answers the God-sized hunger with which each of us is born. This book, too, is for them, a way of coming at the idea of being Catholic *as if* for the first time.

Those longest away will find "the Church" has changed a great deal. It is surely not the unbending hierarchical institution I myself was introduced to a half-century ago. There is much more "give" in the Church and in church people than there was then, much more heartfelt encouragement to read Scripture, to figure doctrinal problems out for oneself and come to a personally validated conclusion. On the local level, the parish is much more a serving community, a segment of "The People of God," missioned by Christ just as much as the clergy, no longer merely an "us" who follow "them." In this sense, returning to full involvement in the Church is slightly more unnerving than it was long ago. The members are no longer "sheep" but fellow shepherds.

Very often books such as this, which try to explain—or reexplain—the basics of Catholicism, seem overly concerned with thoroughness of coverage of all doctrines as if they all carried the same weight, and very often theology forgets to take into consideration the complexity and obscurity of it all, like trying to teach calculus without basic arithmetic. In the interest of logical progression and all-inclusive thoroughness, we teach catechetics (a summary of Christian doctrines and principles) and completely bypass apologetics (Why should I even bother with God, much less with Christianity, and even less with Catholicism and "all those rules"?). We act as if the interested person has already been fully converted and cares to probe further, which is like explaining the intricate mysteries of the internal combustion engine to someone who's not too sure yet whether he even wants to drive.

Religious conversion is much more like falling in love. Hardly ever is it "Wham! Bam! Alacazam! Wonderful you came by!" Maybe in being-in-love songs, but not in real life, which is where most of us live. Here, it usually begins with, "He looks interesting," and "She's cute." Then comes the hard part: just saying hello. The process from that moment to the wedding—and far beyond that— is dramatic only in rare moments, and not all of them pleasant. Like falling in love and only gradually moving to greater and deeper commitment, conversion is a process with its ups and downs.

Saint Paul, on his way to Jericho to root out more Christian heretics, was apparently struck down and overwhelmed by an experience of the risen Jesus. Such conversions are rare indeed. By far, the majority of conversions are far slower and much less dramatic. I'm a cradle Catholic, but my experience of the conversion which was the call of my vocation was surely not that stunning—and by no means that clear and certain. Of all the words in the Gospel, what I find most difficult to accept is that when Jesus stopped by the future apostles' boats and said, "Come, follow me," they "*immediately*" left their nets and followed him. Unless they had considerable previous dealings with Jesus (and the Gospels at least don't say they did), that is *really* hard to accept. I mean, there these hard-handed, practical men are, in the middle of a workday, and this tall stranger just tells them to come along, and they *do?* Just like that? No questions like who is this guy, what about my family, where are we going, what we will eat? Not even *why?*

Not me. When I felt the first urges of a vocation, I did exactly what the prophet Jonah did when Yahweh came and told him to go and convert Nineveh: I ran the other way. I knew what that call was asking me to give up, and I avoided it in every way I knew how for two years. The poet Francis Thompson was also a born Catholic but, swamped among the dregs of humanity and self-hatred, he shuddered when he felt the first whispering of the call back to God:

> *I fled Him, down the nights and down the days;*
> *I fled Him, down the arches of the years;*
> *I fled Him, down the labyrinthine ways*
> *Of my own mind; and in the mist of tears*
> *I hid from Him, and under running laughter.*
>
> *(The Hound of Heaven)*

I don't think too many cradle Catholics understand how conversion feels, what it costs. Perhaps many born-and-baptized, lifelong Catholics have never really suffered a genuine conversion. The faith has simply always been unquestionably true.

The word "conversion" means a total reversal of direction, a *metanoia*, a complete turnabout in one's understanding of what life is all about. The prodigal son, starving among his employer's swine, understood. Oedipus the King, finally yielding to the truth about himself and the gods, understood. Thomas Merton and Dorothy Day understood. Any man or woman who has sinned and repented understands, but so do men and women who have tried their best to live upright lives but—suddenly or gradually—begin to suspect, "I wonder if I could be missing something." It's a *temptation*, and often one that seems to have more drawbacks and uncertainties than assurances.

Other textbooks I have studied that were written to help prepare for the Rite of Christian Initiation of Adults, for welcoming back "vacationing Catholics," for preparing young people for Confirmation, seem (at least to me) to be coming "from the top down," as if those asking for (or submitting to) instruction were completely convinced and docile. As if there were no hesitancies or doubts. On the contrary, I'd like to offer an approach that doesn't jump into the middle, that starts from scratch, that presumes nothing more than, "Yes, uh, I'm mildly interested."

Someone wise once said that skeptics make the best preachers, and that's the way I've written and preached all my adult life. Unlike too many homilists, I never take an audience for granted; I never presume their interest. I learned that from directing ninety plays and musicals (so far), and from thirty years of teaching theology to skeptical high-school seniors, college freshmen, and adults. I never presume they listened to what they were taught before or thought it valuable enough to remember, much less that they accepted it and internalized it. So at every gradual step of the way in this text, I hope you'll face the questions as I have, skeptically. "Now wait just a minute, how can he say that?" After all, this process is asking you to reassess the basic values of your life.

In one *Peanuts* strip, Charlie Brown says to Snoopy who's typing on top of his doghouse, "I hear you're writing a book on theology. I hope you have a good title." And as Charlie walks away, Snoopy says, "I have the perfect title. *Has It Ever Occurred to You That You Might Be Wrong?*" Unless you've honestly examined ideas that challenge your own ideas, you can never be confident in them. If there are five ways of getting a job done, and you know only one way, you don't take that way freely—because it's the only one you know. At the end of this process, I would hope we would no longer be talking about *the* faith, but about *your* faith.

So this text starts a long way before the place most texts for Christian initiation or returning begin: with apologetics, not "apology" in the sense of "I'm sorry," but in the sense of a defense of the very basics upon which any relationship with God (religion) founds itself. Presuming nothing but good will and mutual respect between student and teacher, I would like to begin with terms for realities most texts presume we understand: faith, soul, pride, conscience—as if we all knew what we meant, even the teachers. Let's have at least tentatively satisfying under-standings of what these fundamental realities are and what responses they call for, before we start barging into problems like the validity of Scripture and the nature of the sacraments.

We face the God question early—not the Catholic God or the Christian God or the Muslim God or the Jewish God. Entertain the most basic challenge: What if the atheists are actually right? What if there is no God, objectively, factually, truly? How would our lives be changed if we had the courage to reject what atheists believe is our "crutch"? (*Has It Ever Occurred to You that You Might Be Wrong?*) What hard evidence can we discover to prove that there is a greater likelihood that God exists than that God doesn't? Even if there is a God, why organized religions? Why can't we each go out into the woods and worship God gratefully in our own individual way? If communal worship is better, why not Hindu, Buddhist, Muslim? Why Christian? When asked their core beliefs, most Christian educators would answer: "The Apostles' Creed." Before we study what makes Catholics different, how are all Christians alike?

Most books like this work "from the top down," from the doctrine or the magisterium to the interested Christian. For instance, the *Catechism of the Catholic Church* article on holy orders describes its degrees as episcopate, priesthood, diaconate, because that is the direction in which the ministerial power flows, from Peter and the first apostles (pope and bishops), to the priests and to the deacons. I believe most readers are more comfortable working "from the bottom up," from where we stand. Similarly, in an article on the responsibility of the laity in the Church (906), it says that, when they have serious reason to object to something in the Church, they have an obligation "to manifest it to the sacred pastors." When I quote that passage, I omit the word "sacred" because I believe it skews the relationship. To my mind, the laity are sacred, too.

Finally, even if we can prove a strong probability that Jesus Christ was indeed—and still is—a visitation of God into human life, why be Catholic, with "all those rules"?

Only then, I believe, will we be ready and confident, psychologically and spiritually, to say, "All right. I honestly want to find out about the workings of this Catholic Church, what I am committing myself to, where I have confusions, reservations, objections—and how I can honestly, peacefully resolve them. If I become part of this Church, I want to feel 'at home' in it."

In the larger half of the text, we will treat what other such texts treat, but I hope with the same "show-me," down-to-earth attitude. How do the Scriptures mediate truth? What does the

Church mean, and what effective place does each of us have in the People of God? What is the meaning and purpose of each of the seven sacraments? How does the order of the eucharistic liturgy body forth the beliefs of the people of the Church; how does it convey meaning, enliven, sanctify? How can the progression of the liturgical year give a broader perspective and coherence to its weeks and days? And finally (though it is presumed all along), back to the most basic "connection" to God: praying.

Conversion is most definitely not a blind leap into the dark. It is a slow, taxing, enlightening, and, we hope, invigorating process. A process we also hope will never end. And the great truth is that, in the Church, you never have to do it alone.

This book is for adults and becoming-adults. Without being overly technical and scholarly, it is an attempt to open up the life of the soul, the Christian faith, and the Catholic Church to more than mere childlike (or childish) understanding. Saint Paul says, "When I was a child, my speech, feelings, and thinking were all those of a child. Now that I am a man, I have no more use for childish ways" (I Corinthians 13:11). I am no theologian. I am a pedagogue, a popularizer, trying to make complexities comprehensible without making them either too simplistic or too baffling. Skeptic, take my skeptic's hand.

"Go," said Jesus, "your faith has healed you."

—Matthew 10:52

※ 1 ※

UNCERTAINTY: THE MEANING OF FAITH

Before we approach the faith, it's probably wise to examine just what "faith" means—not specifically faith in God, or faith in a particular religion's unique insights into the nature and personality of God, just a better understanding of what the commitment designated by the word "faith" entails. So let's back off a while from what books like catechisms have to say about faith (which is often pretty heady and inaccessible) and, instead of considering faith "from the top down" the way theologians do, try to understand faith "from the bottom up," starting with acts of faith we're all familiar with. After all, God isn't the only object of faith.

We've all been through the process of forming friendships, but probably never stopped to realize that a friendship is a whole *process* of acts of faith. Think of your very best friend, someone to whom you could unburden anything, who you know without question would stick by you no matter what. Well, at one time, that person was "way out there" in the almost endless sea of anonymous faces— along with old ladies in Manchuria, pygmies in Africa, and the people who tend the boilers in your office building. How did that person get from "way out there" into your innermost heart?

I'm not asking you to explain the atomic theory here, just something we've all experienced but probably never examined. Maybe lay the book aside a few moments and try to figure out how that precious friendship "happened."

The absolutely essential first step, of course, is to *notice* that person. Without that, he or she will remain irretrievably "way out there." After that, we usually assign the new face and body a name, and he or she becomes an *acquaintance*: "Oh, yeah. I know who she is." Most of the people we "know" are acquaintances. But a few people push forward, impressing (or imposing) themselves, spending time together and talking so that they become *friends*—not pals or buddies, just people we don't mind sitting with at lunch. Some penetrate our defenses even further, offering not just time and talk and mutual interests but sacrifice for one another in a common project. That sacrifice tightens the relationship. They become *pals,* people we just assume we'll go with to lunch or a movie or a game. Still others, though, work their way into our innermost hearts, usually because we've shared some truly daunting experience. *Best friends.* Those few become people whom we trust "implicitly"—not blindly, but because of all that shared risk beforehand, *based on* all that previous experience. Those are the people we trust enough to cry with, and know that the tears are not a threat but a kind of cement to the bond of friendship.

Marriage is also an act of faith. In fact, marriage is not just the dramatic commitment at the altar but also an uncountable *series* of acts of faith. It begins from the very first date, when he sits at the intimidating telephone, wiping his palms on his pants, trying to get up the courage to dial ("Oh, God, she won't even remember who I *am!*"), and when he finally gets through, she sits with her eyes squinched and her fillings fused, hesitating ("He's nice, but he's got *braces!*"). The acts of faith—and the risks—multiply in number and escalate in intensity as they go through the years of dating, to the commitment to an engagement, through the formal act of faith at the wedding. Even then they don't *know* it's going to work out; they're *betting* it will. Faith.

And that's by no means the last of it. After the (more-or-less) bliss of the honeymoon, when reality stops by in the form of unpayable bills, ingrained habits at cross purposes, career conflicts, and all the other frictions that naturally arise when two once-autonomous individuals try to form a partnership, then they have to face the *real* act of faith: loving one another without the supportive help of thumping hearts, lusty urges, and the "love potion" that once made her Cinderella and him Prince Charming. That's when romance can turn into love, which is considerably less dramatic than being in love: stirring-the-pasta-sauce love, "No, I'll get up and change her" love, letting-go-of-the-grudge love. In a very true sense, that is probably an even more profound and gradual transition to genuine faith than the actual wedding.

Later, there is the titanic act of faith in having a child—committing themselves to another human being for the next twenty-plus years—and to raising a quarter million dollars (each) to support "it"—sight unseen, and without any chance of an exchange! Then, week after week, there are acts of faith: investments, job changes, school choices—*ad infinitum*. On the couple's thirtieth anniversary, they are *a lot* more married than they were on their wedding day! Because of all those acts of faith—trusting one another through thick and thin, titanic and trivial, that faith becomes incremental; each new act of faith is easier because of all those acts of faith given and fulfilled.

At least for me, this gives a more solid basis for understanding faith than the dictionary definition: "Belief that is not based on proof." If you had proof, what need would there be for belief? Seeing isn't believing, seeing is *knowing*. It's also better than the Pauline one, faith is "the substance of things hoped for." In my waning years, I think I have a better insight into the difference between "faith" and "hope." Hope is the gut urge to cling on even though all the evidence seems to *undercut* it; faith is the gut urge to cling on even though the evidence for it is persuasive but not *compelling*.

A lifetime of belief has convinced me that real, genuine, authentic faith still *doubts*. It *must* doubt. Otherwise, it's not faith but witless conformity. When I ask people what faith means, almost without exception they say, "a blind leap in the dark." Just think for a minute what a "blind leap in the dark" really means. Putting your life's savings on a single lottery ticket is a blind leap. Buying land in Mexico sight unseen is a blind leap. "Hi, we've just met; let's get married" is a blind leap. And they're preposterous. If that's what they think faith is—holding hands and jumping off a cliff—then it's not surprising that having faith is so difficult.

What's more, that "blind leap" business flies directly in the face of what we know from our own personal experience about those other acts of faith—friendship and marriage. Those acts of faith are most often not arrived at logically, but neither are they completely impulsive. And though they may not be painstakingly rational, they are by no means *irrational*. At each stage of the journey of friendship and marriage, when the relationship calls for a deeper commitment and a more profound level of trust, the new commitment is not baseless (like a blind leap), but rather *based on* all their previous experiences together. The same with God.

At the other end of the spectrum from those who say faith is a totally irrational, baseless leap in the dark, there are those who say, "Okay, I'll believe if you can give me scientific proof." They'll commit only when they have ironclad guarantees, evidence so clear and distinct they can have no occasion whatever to doubt it, certitudes as unarguable as water freezing at 32 degrees Fahrenheit (at sea level), objects released from a height going down, and the inevitability of death.

Just as the relativist "blind leap" people labor under a conviction about faith that's irrational, the rationalist "certitude" folks labor under a conviction about faith that's impossible. Even in the cases mentioned: Someone might have dumped antifreeze into the water this time; the object dropped from a great height might be jet-propelled. The only unquestionable certitude in life is death, and even that's unpredictable.

In physics, the "hardest" of the hard sciences, we've known since before Heisenberg won the Nobel Prize in 1932 for his Principle of *Un*certainty that objects in the sub-atomic world simply don't yield to that kind of certitude. You can tell where an electron is located at the moment, but you can't tell its velocity at the same time, because when you bounce a bundle of energy off it to tell where it is, you change its velocity and direction! Sometimes the electron acts like a pellet, sometimes like a wave. Which is it at the moment? Well, uh, we don't know. That's not theology; that's the best of science.

This misconception of "scientific proof" comes, I believe, from the fact that most of us never took anything more than very rudimentary science classes. The "experiments" we did were not experiments at all in the real sense of that word: a tentative procedure to see if something works. The lab manuals were books of *recipes*: If you just don't mess up, this will come out exactly the same every time. Cookbook science. When a real scientist goes into her lab, she doesn't expect to find the cure for the common cold by the time the bell rings, or by the end of the term, or even by the end of her career. Real scientists are content with knowing just a bit more, with pushing back the frontiers of knowledge just a bit more—*exactly* in the same way as people learning to become better friends and better marriage partners. Exactly like establishing faith in God.

Even science, then, is an *act of faith!* It begins with preparation in the rudiments of science. Then, given that knowledge, the scientist gets a hunch: "Maybe if we fiddled with this bread mold we might come up with a medicine; we'll call it penicillin. . . . Maybe if we fooled around with these silicon chips we might find a kind of conductor. . . . Maybe out of this mountain of pitchblende we could get just a small vial of radium."

Those who study the way the human brain works discover two quite different—but complementary—avenues to the truth, two mental functions isolated (more or less) to the left and right lobes. The *left brain* is analytical—taking things apart: rational, logical, organized, working in definitions and formulas; the *right brain* is intuitive—seeing things whole: insightful, engaging in hunches, operating in seeming "leaps," working in symbols, pictures, stories. Each function is vital for a fuller, richer, less simplistic view of what's really out there. In the cases mentioned above, the scientist gets a right-brain "hunch" about the bread mold and silicon and pitchblende and then turns that intuition over to the left brain to see if it does in fact work out rationally and physically. The two functions complement one another.

If one were to work exclusively with the operations of the analytical left brain, for instance, there could be no such thing as friendship and love. Getting married and having children would be utterly foolish without guarantees. Integrity, patriotism, honesty, and humor simply wouldn't compute. All judgments of human behavior would be Puritan, unbending, merciless. Conversely, if one were to work exclusively with the operations of the intuitive right brain, any opinion would be self-justifying, without any need to back it up with evidence; everybody would be going off haphazardly in all directions at once. All judgments of human behavior would be random, wishy-washy, and spineless.

Therefore, the two lobes of the brain need one another to achieve a balanced look at the truth—no matter what the question. To neglect either the rational powers of the left brain or the intuitive powers of the right brain is to act half-wittedly. To say that faith requires absolute certitude or that it is a blind leap without any evidence at all is . . . well, half-witted.

An act of faith (in no matter what) is therefore *neither* a commitment on certitude *nor* an irrational leap. Rather, it's a bit of both: a *calculated risk,* an educated guess, a well-reasoned hunch. Both elements are essential for a well-rounded opinion: the calculated-educated-reasoned part and the risk-guess-hunch part. You will almost never have certitude (about anything), but you come to a point where you have to make a commitment—on a college, a career, a spouse, a child, an investment, God. You gather all the evidence and advice you can (the calculation part) and then you come to a point where you have a hunch that it all just "feels right" (the risk part). Then at least for a while you have to give yourself to the decision to find if it is, in fact, right.

In the case of friendship, one takes a greater risk at each stage of the relationship, often trusting the other *before* one is really *certain* the other is up to it. The same is true of marriage and the scientist in her lab: Each act-of-trust fulfilled provides an even firmer basis from which to take the next leap. There is a risk, all right, just as it was for Olympic diver Greg Louganis when—unthinkably—he cracked his head on the concrete high platform. After he was patched up, he climbed the ladder and dove again. It was a leap, all right, but it wasn't a *blind* leap. It was based on the advice of his coaches, the approval of his doctor, and those countless thousands of other successful dives. It was an act of faith: a calculated risk.

Most of us would like things clear: either/or. But reality fails to conform to our desires (one more proof that *we* are not God). For example, philosophers have always neatly defined humans as "rational animals." Far too simplistic, too reductionist, leaving out evidence which is not only crucial but which definitively separates us from other animals that also have bodies and brains. There are distinctively human activities that simply cannot be reduced to "rational" or to "animal," to body or brain or a combination of the two: unselfish sacrifice even for people we dislike, honor when one could easily get away with something, the need for purpose and meaning, understanding, wisdom, good humor in the middle of terror. All these constitutively human activities (which no other animal has) defy reduction to body or brain. They are solid evidence of a third human power: the soul. And that's where faith "happens."

The principle of *Complementarity* requires a greater tolerance for ambiguity than many people are able to muster. They want clear simplicities. The novel *Lord of the Flies,* for instance, agrees with Martin Luther that human beings are basically savage beasts, held in control only by the structures and strictures of organized society. The first third of any tabloid newspaper gives ample evidence of that truth. Conversely, the novel *A Catcher in the Rye* agrees with Jean-Jacques Rousseau that human beings are angelic innocents corrupted by that very same society. Stories of sublimely noble and nontypical humans like Mother Teresa, Terry Anderson, Nelson Mandela, and Helen Keller give ample evidence for that truth, too. Year after year, students say the two aforementioned books really "tell it like it is"—even though they are completely at *odds* with one another. But the students are right. Because human beings are indeed *both*—at once. Complementarity. Even if the two assertions seem contradictory, you can understand human beings better if you "allow" them to be not either/or but both/and.

Is an electron a pellet or a wave? Yes. Are humans beasts or angels? Yes. Are the operations of the left brain or right brain more important? Yes. Is God utterly otherworldly (transcendent) or utterly this-worldly (immanent)? Yes. Is God three or one? Yes. Was Jesus God or Man? Yes. Are the elements of the Eucharist bread and wine or body and blood? Yes.

If you deal with God exclusively with your prove-it left brain or exclusively with your blind-leap right brain, you'll quite likely never find God. Or at least the God most religions know.

What this book attempts to do is lessen the precariousness of the commitment in faith to a Person you cannot see, whom you cannot box into a definition or into a picture. We can and will explore the strictly rational evidence for and against a Mind Behind It All: the calculation. But just as in the case of friendship and marriage, this calculation can't compel assent. If God is going to "prove" himself, God can do that only in the way your other friends "prove" themselves: noticing, sharing time and talk, sacrificing for one another, trusting one another at rock bottom.

This is the journey we begin.

Questions to Ponder and Discuss

✤ The late film critic Gene Siskel used to ask subjects of interviews: "What are you sure of?" It's a fine question. Myself, I'm sure I'm a flawed good man who tries his best. I'm sure I was born to be a teacher. I'm not at all sure of the causes of original sin, but I'm completely sure of its effects. I'm sure I will not convince all— or even many—to reject their self-absorption, fears, and shortcomings in order to become even more alive *human* beings, much less Christians, much less Catholics. And I'm content with that. What are you sure of?

✢ Further, you know *that* you are sure of certain truths about yourself and your life. For instance, that honor is more important than dishonor, kindness better than exploitation. Can you explore what brings you to these convictions? How did they evolve? Surely not overnight. Try to apply your insights into that process to what lies ahead in trying to become "sure" about God, about organized religion, about Christianity, and about the Catholic Church.

✢ Each of us holds certain values, without which we probably couldn't get through life. Brainstorm, in no particular order at the moment, the values you hold with greatest conviction: Honesty? Ambition? Responsibility? Security? Dignity? Creativity? Then, if it's possible, put them in rough order of priority for you personally. They tell a great deal about you and about the person you bring to God. Mull over the people, the crises, the challenges, the unexpected opportunities that have brought you to where you are as a person now. This surely didn't happen completely by chance, nor did it come about from scrupulous planning. How does one come to know and trust and respect one's own self?

✢ Some people, just because of their upbringing, are shy, hesitant, reserved. Others are outright paranoid, fearful of trusting anyone, anytime. Still others, with enviable confidence, can stride through the jaws of hell without batting an eye. Where do you assess yourself along the spectrum between those two extremes? How easy/difficult is trust for you as a unique person?

✢ What are the obstacles, if any, within yourself to trusting others? What are the hesitancies (and there surely must be some) in trusting God? Many people seem to have a quite satisfying relationship with God without recourse to any organized religion. What are the advantages and disadvantages of sharing a common belief in ritual and community rather than one-on-

One, person-to-Person with God? (Again, surely there are both pluses and minuses; surely a private connection to God and a common connection to God do not preclude one another.)

⚜ If you are exploring these questions with a group, like a parish discussion group or with an RCIA team, how does this process call on your own personal trust in them—and in yourself?

⚜ Thomas Aquinas defines faith as "an act of the intellect assenting to the divine truth by command of the will, moved by God through grace" (II-II, 2,9). Does this "do it" for you? How would you change it to reflect your own experience of faith in others, in marriage, in God?

⚜ It's perfectly okay that you have hesitations about statements from the Fathers of the Church, the present-day administration of the Church, even with Jesus himself—as long as you find some *honest* way to resolve these difficulties, a way which keeps in mind not only your discomforts with a particular saying but also with the powerful source of the saying itself. If you feel such hesitations, bring them up with a priest or religious educator and try to make peace with them, rather than let them rankle. Don't be afraid to ask questions. This is why God gave us minds.

⚜ Scripture: Genesis 22:1-13; Mark 9:14-29; John 6:66-69; Hebrews 11:1-40

⚜ *Catechism:* 199, 1816, 2087-2089

Richard, it profits a man nothing to give his soul for the whole world. *But . . . for* Wales.

—Thomas More, *A Man for All Seasons*

✴ 2 ✴

THE FIRST CONVERSION: HUMANITY

It is a cliché that the purpose of the Catholic Church is "to save our souls" through the merits of Jesus Christ. Like most clichés, it comes trippingly off the tongue, unexamined. What are we saving souls *from?* Indeed, what are we saving? What *is* a soul?

If you roam the jungles of our cities, it's easy to become disheartened. So many hooded eyes, so many dead-ended faces. People hurrying unsmilingly past, unaware of anything but other insulated bodies, locked into the Walkman and the cell phone. So focused, so businesslike, so efficient, so dehumanized, so soulless. Everywhere you look, ads bastardize the meaning of "value." Nothing is really sacred anymore, not even sex. Especially not sex.

Picture a group of babies on a blanket, sweet-smelling, giggling, exploring one another. Now picture a group of people on a subway, slack-jawed, shrouded in blank indifference, coping. All of those older people were once exactly like those children. What got lost?

A lot of things: vulnerability, curiosity, wonder. It may sound silly at first, but I think the death of the soul—what makes us human—begins around second grade. After the innocent self-absorption of infancy, when parents catered to our every need, the world continued to be fascinating. A three-year-old is startled into wonderment every five minutes even by an empty box, a sway-backed nag, raindrops trickling down a windowpane. Pre-school and kindergarten are intriguing, too, exciting. So is first grade: "Look, Mommy! I can write my own name!"

But after that, we've got them. Learning now becomes a serious, efficient business, pointing toward those SATs—and beyond to the dog-eat-dog, it's-a-jungle-out-there, rat-race world. Don't ask questions or make waves. You get *that* material. Don't ask why. It's *required*. The kids who still retain their curiosity, still have hunches, smell rats, ask "Why?" become colossal headaches because they get in the way of the syllabus. Education—real learning, being curious, following the truth wherever it leads, reasoning on your own—yields to schooling, whose sole purpose is to get into a good college so you can get a good job. "This is the way the system works!" But at least by seventh grade, you've learned how to *beat* the system: *CliffsNotes,* the Internet, faked outlines. That's life: beating the system, doing the minimum, getting by. You tread water, and tread water, and tread water. Then you die.

"Is that all there is?"

The sole purpose of education ought to be mastering the

skills to answer the only truly important questions: What are people *for?* What will help me live a truly fulfilled life? What does "success" *really* mean? I have only one time around; how do I get the most from it?

When I was applying to the Society of Jesus, I wrote in my letter that I wanted to become a Jesuit "in order to save my soul and the souls of others." How enviably naive I was. Then, I pictured myself like Holden Caulfield in *A Catcher in the Rye*, standing at the brink of a literal hell, trying to save others (and myself) from eternal fire. Now, I struggle might and main to keep as many souls as I can from withering into atrophy here and now.

The Soul

It may seem odd at first, but no one sees you. The real you—your true self—is invisible. All anybody sees is your body. They watch how you use your body, hear the kinds of things you talk about and are important to you, and make *educated guesses* about who the real you is. But that's all they are, just guesses, and often not too "educated." Even you might be hard-pressed to "capture" yourself in words on paper. Your real self—your soul, your who-I-am, the essence that grounds all the disparate parts of you—is elusive. You can't catch it on an x-ray plate or analyze its chemical components. And yet it really is *there*. As we saw before, your soul is the root of all those crucial qualities and processes that can't be reduced to the body or the brain, that we share with no other animals: unselfish love, honor, dreams, hopes, freedom, dignity, humor. Faith.

There are several ways of studying that soul/self—as the enlivening *force* that animates our bodies and (we hope) continues after the body is no longer needed, as the *humanity* in us which joins us to all other humans, as the *personality* each of us projects to those outside (extrovert/introvert, confident/shy, artistic/rational), as the *character* (conscience) that embodies a whole scheme of values and principles which gives a sense of integrity and rootedness to one's life, and as the *spirit*—which is the soul, fully alive—the *super*natural self, not "super" in the sense of above or heavenly but in the sense of "superenergized."

Our Life Force. You know someone is still alive when their breath fogs a mirror. In Hebrew, Greek, and Latin the word for "breath" is the same word for "soul": *ruah, pneuma, anima.* When someone dies, something real that was there before is gone; the body is there, but the *person* is not. Most cultures have believed that, although the body dies and decays, that human and individual essence lives on—because of the very fact it *is* immaterial. Thirty thousand years ago, neanderthals buried their dead with weapons and provisions, because they believed the soul—the person—was on a journey into another way of existing.

Our Humanity. All of us are human beings, and therefore you can learn more about "what people are for" from every book you read. Since the Cro-Magnons, we have each and all gone through exactly the same stages of human life: birth, weaning, play years, learning the skills of the tribe, agonizing through adolescence, falling in love, marrying (or not), having children (or not), losing parents, growing old, dying. And every human from the start has faced the same temptations that arise from yoking an abstractive cerebral cortex to an Id-ridden body: pride, covetousness, lust, anger, gluttony, envy, and sloth—among others. Everyone's story can enliven our stories, allow us to share and learn from their experiences without suffering their scars.

Our Personality. Yet each of us is also unique; we've gone through the same processes and faced the same temptations in a singular, never-repeated way. Who am *I?* Well, I'm a sixty-ish white, American priest from Buffalo, who went to these seminaries, and taught in these places, and wrote these books." Yes. But who are *you?*

One might guess that most people are really "accidental selves." Each has a personality—habits of coping with others instinctively learned before age three in reaction to parents and siblings. A first child of inexperienced parents, for instance, might unthinkingly respond to their apprehensions by trying to be the best little boy or girl ever, anal-retentive, self-critical (without the ability to reason yet), introverted. A second child of the same parents might see what a bag of nerves the first one's become and react in the opposite way: extroverted, demanding, stubborn. Neither personality type is better or worse, and no child is responsible for which one he or she is. But each of us *is* responsible for what we *make* of what we've been left with. Personality isn't an incurable disease (as in "I'm just a procrastinator" or "I push in and get my way; that's the way I am"). The shy person can develop confidence; the aggressive person can learn to be reflective.

Our Character. Personality is automatic; we made no effort to determine it, though we might well expend the effort to change it. Character (as we will see more fully in the next chapter) is by no means automatic. There is no doubt we're socialized by parents, schools, and the media to accept certain principles (what Freud called the superego) without question, just as we unwittingly adopted personalities. But psychologists all agree the purpose of adolescence is to take charge of one's own Id, critique the strictures unquestioningly taped in the superego, and evolve an Ego—a *personally* validated moral self. Many don't do that, primarily because they've never been encouraged to do it by the people who claim to be preparing them for life. Thus, so many become "accidental selves," made up of mismatching and often contradictory views picked up from hither and yon. That, too, can be remedied, but only after a great deal of soul-searching.

Our Spirit. Spirit is to the soul as the flame is to the candle. It is the soul fully alive, as the title *Buddha* means "The One Fully

Awake." We've all known people who just seem to be bursting apart with life, people who—like cats—seem to stuff nine lives into one. There's almost an intensity or power or aura that emanates from them: Mother Teresa, Pope John XXIII, Carol Burnett, Robin Williams, Oprah Winfrey. "Spirituality" is one's soul-life, and a gratifying number of people of all religious persuasions are now studying ways to ignite their souls.

When Claire Booth Luce was considering becoming a Catholic, she said she used to look at Catholics, especially seminarians, and ask herself: "You say you have the truth. Well, the truth should set you free, give you joy. Can I *see* your freedom? Can I *feel* your joy?"

Nifty questions for anyone considering Catholicism to ask.

The Potential Soul

The soul is unquestionably "there," but it is only *potential*. It needn't be activated.

marble : acorn = cub : baby

At first, both of those pairs seem relatively similar. The marble and acorn are about the same size and heft, but actually they're a quantum leap apart. Plant them both, and the marble is just going to lie there; it's incapable of being anything other than itself. But the acorn has the potential to be hugely different: an enormous oak. Or not. If it lands in a swamp, it rots; if it falls on a sidewalk, it dries up. But given the right conditions, it can become unbelievably different from what it started out as. The same is true of the cub and the baby (except the baby has less hair): both about the same size, eating, sleeping, excreting, exploring. But, again, there is an enormous difference in potential. Both the cub and the baby will become larger, but the cub is never going to become more vulpine or ursine. The baby, though, has the potential to become Helen Keller or Thomas Jefferson. Or not. He or she can land in a hardscrabble patch of the country, and dry up—though there is always a chance, as with Abraham Lincoln. Or he or she can land in the lushness of an upper-class suburb and rot into a druggie. But if the conditions are right—and if the individual reacts courageously to the challenges—he or she can become an incandescent soul.

So the term "humanity"—soul—is another spectrum, ranging from pimps, pushers, and terrorists at one end (just over the line from animals) all the way to great souls like Thomas More and Joan of Arc. The purpose of humanistic education (as opposed to schooling for a job) is to lure us along that spectrum as far as we feel we are able to go. And then a touch further.

The people in that subway car, the people who sourly make change for them, the surly girl at the checkout counter, the empty selves who spray graffiti on walls to prove they exist, the drive-by shooters, the functionaries in concentration camps who processed children like trash, didn't really "sell" their souls or even "lose" them. They never even took possession of them.

The first step in enlivening the soul/self is to admit one even has one—or, rather, *is* one. I don't "have" a soul, I "am" a soul. The soul is all that I truly am. Then one has to commit oneself to evolving it, becoming more truly human, exercising the two powers which only humans have: learning and loving. The more I open myself to understanding the world and people, the more I am vulnerable to the needs of others, the more human I become. One needs to take time to experience the self, to ignite it, to expand it. The alternative is withering into atrophy as a self.

Near the end of his life, Dr. Sigmund Freud enunciated an idea he called The Pleasure Principle. He said that any human life is governed by one of two principles: Eros, the life wish, or Thanatos, the death wish. Eros craves challenge; Thanatos craves security. Eros is what gets us out of bed in the morning, leaving behind the warm womb of the blankets in the hope of finding something better, more enriching, even at the cost of risking a loss. Thanatos craves being unbothered, the minimum, "just leave me alone, and I'm fine," the paradise embodied in South Seas travel posters. It's Eros that impels us to do more than "the written stuff," that reaches further than we'd dared, that gets married, that has children, that changes course, that takes a chance on God. It's Thanatos that huddles on the couch before the anesthetizing TV, that says, "I'm too old for that," that settles for routine and the status quo—in fact, fights for it.

Self-Esteem and Narcissism

Again, at the risk of oversimplification, in thirty-eight years of teaching, I can't think of a single personal problem ever brought to me—an A mind with C grades, acting out, consistent discipline problems, cheating, lying, vandalism, unwanted pregnancy, suicide—which wasn't reducible to a lack of honest, legitimate self-esteem.

Slipshod translation has always rendered the Greek word *hubris* as "pride," as in "Pride goeth before the fall" or "Those whom the gods would smite, they first make proud." For a Greek, *hubris* didn't mean honest pride in a job well done, the weary admission that today I didn't knock 'em all dead, but I' by God did my best. It meant *arrogance*—the self-absorptive narcissism of Oedipus, Napoleon, Hitler—rejecting the need for others, even—or especially—the gods. As a result, countless thousands of good people, trying their best, have been afraid to be proud, lest they be accused (or accuse themselves) of vanity.

Narcissism—self-absorption, hubris, vanity—never goes to confession nor feels the need to. In fact, honestly confessing weakness is utterly repellent. Narcissists tell themselves lies about themselves, and—worse—*believe* them. "I'm an honest person. I cheat only when I have need and opportunity." "I'm okay, a good person. So I don't give an honest day's work for an honest day's pay. Who's not human, right?" The Greek root of "narcissism" is the same as the root for "narcotic": *narkoun,* "to benumb." Narcissists are dulled to the needs and feelings—and often even the very existence—of other people. It's narcissism that sprays graffiti, revs up the boom box, spits gum in the drinking fountain, leaves the toilet roll empty.

Unlike the narcissism natural in children, which has to be challenged in adolescence, honest self-esteem is based on a legitimate conviction of personal worth. That conviction is legitimized by the *inner* self: I am responsible for what I do, for what I say, for who I am. I appreciate the support of my friends; I honestly entertain their criticisms; but even without the support of those I honestly love, I can stand alone if I must. There are scars on my soul left by others, by my own stupid mistakes and cowardice, but I take responsibility for what happens to the rest of my life. I am responsible to the truth, without illusions or vested interests. I am as rigorously honest with my self as I can be. What I "must" do has become what I "want" to do.

No one with genuine self-respect would ever degrade themselves to lie or cheat or do a halfhearted job or fall for easy, casual sex. Character—conscience, self-possession, ego, soul—is the inner compass that steers us through the storms. Perhaps the key virtue of all is complete and unbiased honesty with oneself, about oneself. After that, it's all improvisation.

Questions to Ponder and Discuss

❧ Each of us knows enviable people who seem to be "full-souled," people who seem to have life by the tail, people whose freedom we can see and whose joy we can feel. Pick one of these people and reflect on him or her. How do their freedom and joy manifest themselves *concretely*, in their actions, habits, choices, responses to others? There's a difference between someone who is manic, daredevil, frenetic, and someone who at least appears to live life every minute. What goes into developing the wisdom to be serene in the face of "the things that can't be changed" and the courage to change "the things that can be changed"?

❧ Every life is governed by Eros, the life wish that craves challenge, or by Thanatos, the death wish that craves security. Reflect awhile, honestly, which urge governs your own life. It's easy to waffle the question: "Well, in things I enjoy, I operate under the life wish; with jobs and people I find taxing...." Overall, at the root, do you *find* life where most other people find tedium? Do you *infuse* life into the detestable jobs? Martin Luther King Jr. said, "If your job is to sweep streets, sweep those streets the way Michelangelo would have swept them." The poet Kahlil Gibran wrote that, if you have to make a chair, make one for your beloved to sit in. Psychiatrist Viktor Frankl said that, even in the concentration camps, the prisoner still had the ultimate human freedom: his or her *attitude*.

❧ Whenever I hear confessions, I always end up with, "You're a good person, aren't you?" Almost invariably the embarrassed response is, "Well, I try to be" or "I hope so" or "You really don't know me that well." Of course, there's only one honest answer to that question. Bad people don't come to confession; only good people do; bad people—narcissists—don't think they need to. So the mere fact they have the honesty with themselves to confess their faults to another human being (and God) proves beyond argument that they're good people—trying. But good people are almost always also hyperaware of vanity. Can you, in your most honest heart, say, "I'm a good person. Thank God I'm me"? It's the only "me" you're ever going to have. If you keep knocking that self, upbraiding it for each of its shortcomings and imperfections, you're not likely to challenge it to the greatness you were born for.

❧ No doubt, life is a serious business. Bills to pay, family to worry about, deadlines to meet, enigmas, expectations. How often do you pull off the road, out of the rat race in which so many can begin to *feel* like rats? In what ways do you nourish and challenge your soul? Jesus said that unless we become as little children, we will never even find the Kingdom of God. Where do you go to re-enliven your sense of wonder, curiosity, awe?

❧ Some truly great souls—like the Buddha, Jesus, John the Baptist, Mohammed—found their true human potential, their connection to the Ultimate, alone in the desert or on a mountaintop. But such courageous souls are few. What are the advantages in seeking to understand our souls with other seekers? Especially with others committed enough to the effort to offer their time to share the search with you? What dimension does this search take on when it reaches beyond the everyday into eternity?

❧ Scripture: Psalm 42:1-3; 131:1-3; Luke 1:46-55; 11:33-36; Matthew 10:27-29; 16:25-27

❧ *Catechism:* 363-368

Character is who you are when no one is watching.

—Victor Steele

✻ 3 ✻

CONSCIENCE

As far as we know, no shark gobbles up a swimmer and fins back into the depths of the ocean muttering, "Oh, God! I did it *again!* I need counseling!" No other species we know suffers pangs of guilt; only we do. There is no such thing as a bad rock; if it falls on someone, it's no more "responsible" than the dumb force of gravity is. There is no bad cabbage; if it spoils, it's only obtusely following the laws of chemistry. There is no bad dog; if it wets the rug, it's only "doin' what comes natcherly." (Not bad dog, lazy owner.) But humans do act *against* their nature, which is to learn and to love. No wolf refuses to act vulpine; no pig refuses to act porcine. But humans refuse to act humanly; they treat themselves and others as no better than beasts, or mindless vegetables, or stepping-stones. In fact, original sin is about the only doctrine you can prove from any tabloid newspaper.

Conscience differentiates us from all other species. To put it clumsily, if spirit is the soul's heart, conscience is its mind.

Inborn Conscience

I actually read this statement in a book written to prepare adults for entrance into the Church: "God plants the natural law in our hearts when he creates us. Within our deepest being is a light that comes from God's eternal law and glows within us." If this statement were true, if God plants the natural law in our hearts at the moment of conception, how did we ever get Hitler and Stalin (both of whom were not only created but baptized)? How did we get Nero, Attila the Hun, and Pope Alexander VI? Pimps, pushers, drive-by shooters, mob hitmen, terrorists who blow up school buses? If the natural law is a built-in catechism, why do we need cops, prefects of discipline, and school crossing guards? If the laws of God regarding moral (human) behavior are written in our hearts from birth, it must be in invisible ink. Or in some language no human can discern.

Such books also talk about "Christian morality." But morality means what one must do to be a decent *human* being rather than an animal. Christians have no monopoly on morality. Mohandas Gandhi was probably a saint, but he was a Hindu, not a Christian. Albert Camus struggled to be an integral human being despite his atheism. I suspect most the students I've taught, nearly all of whom equate Christianity and morality, do so simply because the only moral training they've ever had was under Christian auspices.

As we will see more thoroughly later, Christianity goes far, far beyond being human, far beyond ethics and justice, to uncondi-tional selflessness. Christianity is epitomized in the crucifix: a statue of a corpse, utterly used up for others. The Christian says: "There is the most completely fulfilled human being who ever lived, caught at the moment of his greatest triumph. I want to be like him." As Jesus showed, Christianity forgives without the need for atonement.

Conscience is not inborn. Only the *potential* for conscience is inborn, like the humanity it manifests. And just as with humanity, development of one's conscience is a spectrum—again, from pimps and pushers at one end (just above animals, with no conscience at all) all the way to great-souled men and women like Albert Schweitzer and Mother Hale.

The Natural Law

The will of God is not written into our minds or hearts, but it *is* written in the nature of things "out there," and our task as evolving human beings, growing consciences, is to study those natures—mineral, vegetable, animal, and human—and discover how they are made, how they differ, and how each nature governs how we can legitimately use them. The Bible, the doctrines of the Church, the laws of the land, or in fact any book can help us form personally validated consciences. But what determines whether those sources of insight are valid or not is not in the books themselves but in the evidence "out there" that supports their statements.

There really shouldn't be any need for a law forbidding parents brutalizing their children, or drivers speeding 80 mph in a school zone, or graffiti artists defacing other people's property. Any fool ought to be able to see those actions as objectively wrong. Laws are made for dumb people, self-absorbed people, lazy people. The evidence for any just law is right "out there" in the natures of things, in the way in which they're made. Good lawmakers see that evidence and draw up rules for people who can't or won't do that for themselves.

The *rock* comes to me; it tells me what it is and how I can legitimately use it. It has mass, weight, electrical charge, and it just sits there, inert and unfeeling. I can kick it, cut it, mortar it into a wall, use it as a tool. Objective fact.

The *apple* comes to me; it tells me what it is and how I can legitimately use it. It has all the properties of the rock, *but* it can take in food, grow, reproduce—which no rock can do. That's a quantum leap up. And the apple can also feed an animal or human and, because it has no feelings, I can cut it up, boil it, and consume it. But there's something *inside* the apple—a value—which the rock doesn't have; its power to feed makes it objectively unfitting to lob it around in food wars as if it had no more inner value than snowballs. Objective fact.

The *rabbit* comes to me; it tells me what it is and how I can legitimately use it. All the properties of the rock and apple, *but* it can move around, sense danger, feel pain—which no apple can do. That ability to feel pain makes it objectively unfitting to pour alcohol over it and set it afire—as I can legitimately do with a Christmas pudding. But because the rabbit is of a lower species, humans can use its meat to preserve their lives. Objective fact.

Humans come to me; they tell me what they are and how I can legitimately use them. They have all the properties of the rock, the apple, the rabbit, *but* they are self-aware—which, as far as we can see, even the smartest animal is not. They can anticipate the not-yet-real, like death. Most tellingly, only humans have the capacity for conscience. Objective fact.

Therefore—looking at the objective evidence—we see that, although animals are prisoners of their natural programming, humans have a potential no other animal has: the capacity to judge right from wrong—to act humanly, or less than humanly, or inhumanly. So, you can assess whether a human is good— moral—by whether he or she has fulfilled that "humans-only" potential. If a human acts like a beast or treats other humans like beasts, or treats animals like unfeeling toys, or vegetates, or uses other humans as mere stepping-stones, he or she is less than human.

We're not talking about sin here, just about whether you honestly have the right to feel good about yourself.

Moral Evil and Sin

Even atheists, who have no belief in either God or sin, are aware of the pervasiveness of moral evil—antihuman behavior—not only in our own time but throughout human history. Moral evil violates (if you'll allow the very inadequate spacial metaphor) the *horizontal* web of our relationships with other human beings and with our common environment. No one can legitimately yoke human beings to a plow as they could oxen, or do experiments on human beings as they could viruses, or use a human being as third base as they could a rock. It's simply wrong, and that wrongness comes not from some society or church or Scripture. The very nature of a human being manifests its inherent worth. *The Declaration of Independence* states that each of us has a *self-evident right* to life, liberty, and the chance to pursue happiness—not because we are Americans, but because we are human beings. Whether there is a God or not. "Do unto others as you would have others do unto you" is not the private preserve of any particular religion. In fact, if one studies them, every religion and positive philosophy in history has echoed that same need. The Golden Rule is not about relationship with God but a matter of human society's survival.

Sin, on the other hand, violates not only that horizontal web of relationships all humans share but—in the same act—violates a *vertical* relation with God, our creator. In the strictest sense of the word, an honest atheist cannot sin, because there is no vertical relationship with God. A child cannot sin. But both an atheist and a child *can* perpetrate moral evil, antihuman behavior.

Superego: The Temporary Conscience

When a child is born, he or she is pretty much an animal (with the human potential no animal has, a potential which may or may not be activated). For the first year and a half or so, the parents cater to the child's needs as they would to a helpless puppy. But at a very early age, when the child begins naturally to develop muscle control, the parents have to start saying two words the infant has never heard before: "good" and "bad." Once the child can "get into" things, the parents have to impose on the child what Freud called a superego, a list of commands taped without the ability to question by a two-foot person looking up at a six-foot person. The child can't understand why it's okay to bite the bread stick but not the cat's tail; "good" to throw the ball to Daddy but "bad" to throw the spaghetti. But the child accepts those strictures, even when they are—to a critical mind—contradictory, like "love your neighbor" but "don't play with *them.*"

Consider a case where a person has been given *no* superego as a child: the young man a few years ago who went across southern New York State purposely infecting young women with HIV. His grandmother was a crack addict; his mother prostituted herself and her ten-year-old daughter to support her own habit. As a child, he roamed from one crack house to another, with no limits whatsoever on his actions. He is a sociopath, conscienceless, little better than a beast. And if he doesn't have the imposed, temporary, secondhand conscience (a superego), he's very unlikely to evolve his own conscience, validated by the objective natures of things and people.

Further, forty years ago, all the voices in a child's life—parents, schools, peers, media—all chanted the same message onto that superego, the Scout virtues: trustworthy, loyal, helpful, friendly, courteous, kind, obedient, cheerful, thrifty, brave, clean, and reverent. Now, however, since the invention of the Electronic Baby-sitter, far more *contradictory* messages are being taped from the media, rock lyrics, the *playboy-playgirl* mystique. And from all sources—parents/media, religion/peers, school/streetcorner—the messages are taped *uncritically.* They're all "true," even when they blatantly controvert one another. As a result, when asked who their heroes are, more than a few say Mother Teresa *and* Donald Trump. Good luck.

Many say conscience means "a small voice in my head telling me what's right and wrong." Perhaps true, but it's not just one voice but a host of completely *contradictory* voices. "It's honorable to be chaste" *versus* "If you're a virgin at eighteen, you have to be queer—or sick." And for far too many, the superego is not really temporary until the individual is old enough to critique it, but permanent, no matter how self-contradictory. As such, it is always secondhand, even though we call it "my" conscience. As Pirandello wrote, "Don't you see that blessed conscience of yours is nothing but other people inside you?"

In earlier times, the Bible and the Church were the principal elements of the superegos of most predominantly uneducated Catholics, mediated to children through parents, sermons, schools, art, feast days and fast days. As they grew, those truths became the warp and woof of their lives. But as societies became more sophisticated, they became more skeptical about the value of nonutilitarian beliefs. But—and this is a very forceful "but"— if the ordinary man and woman on the street became more skeptical, that doesn't mean they became more intellectually perceptive and honestly critical of their secondhand consciences. Rather, just as adolescents ordinarily break rebelliously away from the beliefs of their parents only to enthrall themselves uncritically to the unquestioned "values" of their peers, now almost all my students (adult as well as adolescent) seem to have removed their consciences from the manipulative influence of

Bible and Church and handed them blithely over to "society."
The reason, of course, is as old as Dostoevski's Grand Inquisitor:
the human fear of freedom. If they didn't allow someone else to
do their thinking for them, they would (God forbid) have to
think for themselves.

Among the people I teach, it is almost axiomatic—and
ineradicable—that "Society decides what's right and wrong, and
then it tells us." Even after a whole year, some still mark true for
"Objective morality changes from age to age and culture to
culture." Things were different fifty years ago; now things
forbidden then are not only allowed but recommended—or even
required.

If objective morality (what it takes to be a decent human)
changes from age to age, Plato has nothing to tell us about being
human. Nor did Jesus, Buddha, Shakespeare, or Dickens. Moral
discourse is little more than verbal Ping-Pong, and libraries are a
terrible waste of money. If any current society decides what's
moral and immoral, hiding Jews in Nazi Germany or runaway
slaves in the antebellum South was immoral. Conversely, slaugh-
tering Inca virgins to placate the gods was laudable in their
society because their society said so.

They were wrong. What allows me to say that? The objective
facts. The humanity of Jews, Blacks, and Inca virgins is no more
debatable than the spherical shape of the earth or the toxicity of
cyanide. Objective fact, no matter what any society or religion or
scripture says. There is a very real and important difference
between "legal" and "moral."

A Spectrum of Consciences

Using such moral dilemmas as deciding whether a poor farmer
could legitimately steal an exorbitantly priced drug for his dying

wife, Lawrence Kohlberg of Harvard developed three separate, deepening levels of moral motivation, depending on the scope of the respondent's human concern, from completely self-centered, to group-centered, to principle-centered. Each level is further divided into two stages.

LEVEL I: PRE-CONVENTIONAL
Id / Child / Self-centered

Stage 1: Fear of Punishment
I'll be good, or they'll punish me.

Stage 2: Hope of Reward
I can gain more by being good.

LEVEL II: CONVENTIONAL
Superego / Parent / Loyalty-centered

Stage 3: Group Loyalty
This group deserves my being good.

Stage 4: Law and Order
Society depends on our being good.

LEVEL III: POST-CONVENTIONAL
Ego / Adult / Principle-centered

Stage 5: Principle
I couldn't live with myself if I didn't do the right thing.

Stage 6: Integrity
I will follow my principles even if they punish me for it.

Level I, the Pre-Conventional, is basically focused on the Id, what Transactional Analysis calls "The Child." Stage 1 of this self-centered level is motivated solely by fear of punishment; Stage 2, one step up, works primarily by hope of reward, no matter if the profit is licit or not.

Level II, the Conventional, is a quantum leap upward, spreading beyond the self to a convinced loyalty to the Superego, what TA calls "The Parent." The individual's awareness and concern reaches *beyond* self-interest—at Stage 3, to small groups like a family, team, platoon, and at Stage 4 to a larger collectivity like nation or Church. It is a personal belief in law and order.

Level III, the Post-Conventional, is another quantum leap upward, basically focused on the rightness of an action in itself, rather than on what is good for oneself or one's group. It goes not against the law but *beyond* the law. It is the stage of the personally validated moral ego, what TA calls "The Adult." The individual's concern moves beyond parochial concerns—at Stage 5 to the whole human family and at 6 to the primacy of personal integrity, even at the price of death.

The levels and stages have nothing to do with educational attainment or age. Kohlberg and his colleagues found morally decent youngsters and illiterates and morally cramped, educated, middle-aged people. Consider Forrest Gump and Rhodes scholar Bill Clinton.

The difference in the levels is that, at Level I, the person says, "My parents would kill me." At Level II the person says, "This would kill my parents." At Level III, "It would kill me to do that, even if my parents asked me to." Moving from Level I to Level II frees the person from the tyranny of the Id; moving from Level II to Level III frees the person from the domination of the superego. Such people would opt for the objectively better moral choice even if all the police in the world went on strike, even if the government ordered them to degrade themselves or die.

Kohlberg and his colleagues also made other discoveries about moral awareness. Perhaps most important is that persons at a given stage cannot even *comprehend* the motivations in moral dilemmas of persons two stages above them. Thus, someone at Stage 2 would find the law-and-order motives of someone at Stage 4 ludicrous. "For a *law?* When you can get *away* with it?"

Even someone at the law and order stage couldn't comprehend the altruism required to face martyrdom for a cause or celibacy in order to serve. Therefore, attempts by those in charge of moral development in the young to motivate behavior by an appeal to the authority of Level II—much less the altruism of Level III—are spinning their wheels. According to the research, the very best one can hope for even as late as senior high school is Stage 4 motivation: law and order.

Kohlberg's conclusions are satisfying, rational, easily schematized. They offer a clear outline of developmental growth and a check on educators' expectations of what is possible. (Though most teachers I know who have read Kohlberg still expect to graduate altruists.) But they are one-sided, incomplete. They need the corrective of the rightbrain, empathic, feminine.

Carol Gilligan, Kohlberg's student, called her mentor to task for being overly rationalistic and "masculine," citing the fact that a disproportionate number of his respondents of all ages were male. One telling incident she reports sums up her objection perfectly. After a session on a moral dilemma, one young boy said, "These dilemmas are just like math problems, only with people."

But people are not numbers, and ethics is not calculus.

Cold-eyed (and coldhearted) analysis is not enough—essential, but only partway. It is helpful to understand *before* the fact that some acts are objectively supremely inhuman, others serious, some trivial. Yet each inhumanity has to be judged *after* the fact in context, with inclusive, "feminine," rightbrain insight. Murder, for instance, is objectively evil, depriving another human being of the supreme right: to life. But most philosophers agree that, if you were set upon by someone with a lethal weapon and had one yourself, you could deprive your assailant of life because, in attempting to deny you life, he or she had surrendered his or her own right to it.

Contrary to the total impartiality one expects from law courts and empirical science, in judging *human* (i.e., moral) problems, one has to include not only the objective moral evil but the specific, unique situation and the perpetrator's context as well—even when the perpetrator is oneself. As Gilligan insists, too often moralists and churchfolk encourage us unselfishly to factor our own selves out of the moral equation, which is manifestly lopsided in favor of the law. What she suggests is not a regression to relativism but an admission of ambiguity.

Once again, complementarity.

Certainly, moral education should provide a hierarchical understanding of moral evils rooted in objective facts in order to equip us with an understanding of those evils *before* the fact of committing one. *After* the fact, if we are to be truly human and not vindictive vultures, we have to temper justice with compassion, no matter what our religious beliefs or lack of them. And if we are followers of the Christ who dealt with the "woman known as a sinner in the town," the adulterous woman, the Samaritan woman at the well, the prodigal son, and the Peter who denied even knowing him three times, we are called to go even further than that. Much further.

Questions to Ponder and Discuss

✦ Many believe—and resent, in a kind of unfocused way—that a law or commandment "makes" an action a sin, as if God one day reared up and said, "What do they really like? Let's forbid it!" Or that the people who wrote the Bible and the people who formulate church laws were all out-of-it celibates who had no real understanding of human beings at all and try to make us as withered and joyless as they are. Manifestly foolish. Was it evil for Cain to slay Abel, even if the Ten Commandments were thousands of years from publication? Of course it was. Why?

✤ We've known since Socrates that the young are as fractious as mavericks under saddle when it comes to restrictions on their freedom. If Kohlberg's research is true, then we also know that the best we can hope for from the young is dutifulness and that they are incapable of valuing the altruistic selflessness of martyrdom or celibacy (or, thus, the crucifixion). Yet our attempts to interiorize moral motives in the Catholic schools and homes has been almost exclusively based on authority ("the Bible says," "the Church says") and altruism (the example of Jesus and the saints). And anyone who has studied the radical changes in values and behavior in the young (and not so young) in the fifty years since Norman Rockwell and Joe DiMaggio can attest that, despite our best intentions, our methods of moral instruction simply don't work. After ten years of what they themselves call "Catholic brainwashing," their motives for moral choices seem little different from those of the decent atheist down the street. Does this mean that any attempts to make our young at least moral human beings are futile? If authoritarian and altruistic motives are at the very best inadequate, what avenues are still open to us?

✤ List each of the levels and stages of Kohlberg's moral development scheme and try to find a character from literature or history or films who clearly falls into that category. This exercise should not only focus the theory more concretely but might also give insights into people you deal with every day, where they are coming from, and what you can legitimately expect of their moral awareness and behavior. Again, what realistic approaches can you imagine which might have a chance of coaxing them just a bit further up the scale?

✢ What one knows from the Bible and from church doctrine and tradition ought to be included, with great weight, into one's formation of a personal conscience. But although the Bible and the Catechism are good books, they are not the *only* books. How does an individual resolve the dilemma when what the Bible and Church clearly say is moral/immoral conflicts squarely with everything else one knows from all kinds of other reliable sources? For instance, the Church resolutely resisted Galileo's sun-centered solar system because it called in question the Bible's infallible claim that the sun stood still. Fundamentalists of all denominations have to suspend disbelief and believe that, at least in the beginning, snakes could talk. Over a very long time, the Church had to go back and reconsider its certitudes, discovering in the end the differences between literal truth and literary truth, between accurate and meaningful. The evangelists wrote not as historians but to *evangelize*, reporting not what eyewitnesses actually saw but what was actually *happening*. If what the Bible/Church say on a particular moral matter seems irresolvable with most of the rest of what you believe, how *do* you resolve the dilemma?

✢ Scripture: 1 Samuel 24:1-23; Romans 12:8-14; Titus 1:15-16; 1 Peter 3:20-22

✢ *Catechism:* 1776-1802

Life's but a walking shadow, a poor player
That struts and frets his hour upon the stage
And then is heard no more; it is a tale
Told by an idiot, full of sound and fury
Signifying nothing.

—Shakespeare, *Macbeth*

❊ 4 ❊

A WORLD WITHOUT ENCHANTMENT: ATHEISM

The Myth of Progress, which so many accept as beyond challenge, is indeed evidenced by longer lives, faster travel, controlled diseases, more leisure. And yet in the geometric rate at which our lives have been improved since the days of the caves—or even since our long, painful trek through the Great Depression and World War II, we have also generated a society in which crimes against children are commonplace, half of new marriages end in divorce, affluent teenagers (and adults) who "have it all" kill themselves, homeless people haunt the streets, and the spread of sexually transmitted diseases now rivals the Great Plague. In a very real sense, the progress of "civilization" has also been a process of dehumanization.

For all our speed and efficiency, for all our goods and services, for all our defenses against even inconvenience, for all our better nutrition and medical care, are we demonstrably happier than the primitive squatting among so many enchantments, the Hebrew clutching his prayer shawl and muttering to Yahweh, the medieval peasant leaning her hoe on the furrow to say the Angelus? Do we have a more genuine sense of self, a more heartfelt sense of belonging to a community and a cause greater than the limits of our own skins, a true sense of living purposeful lives, than those simpler folk, benighted in simplicity, superstition, and magic? Are we missing something?

In primitive cultures, people's lives were surrounded and permeated by gods and rituals in which they found their meaning and purpose, as tribes and individuals, by interacting with the powerful forces of nature. The yearly *rhythm* of natural change gave a rhythm to their own lives—a sense of rightness, wholeness, meaning, like an artfully composed piece of music into which they blended. It gave a center to their lives, a connectedness, a shared vision, a *coherence*.

Today, we can't see the stars for the neon, hear the wind for the Walkmans, or enjoy the view without taking pictures of it, to have proof we were there.

As societies became more sophisticated, as in ancient Greece, the primitive (and surely dysfunctional) gods of Homer became more rarefied into a single Deity, not trapped within this world but infinitely removed from the everyday, a god of rarefied ideals who showed human beings, through reason, what was truly real, good, beautiful. At the same time, in the Far East, wise folk came to the same conclusion: that the world of nature we *believe* is real is a delusion, and the purpose of human life is to deny the material world and aspire to the nonphysical liberation of Nirvana, absorption into the Oversoul.

Meanwhile, along the eastern shore of the Mediterranean, there lived a people of quite different mind-set than their neighbors to the west and east: the Hebrews. They were far less heady, far more down-to-earth. Their relationship with the Source of Life was far "warmer" than the Greek's First Cause or the Hindu-Buddhist's impersonal Oversoul. God was incontestably "other," yet they knew Yahweh also dwelt in the center of their city, in the Temple, transcendent (otherworldly) like the Greek and Indian experience of God, and yet immanent (this-worldly) like far earlier primitive societies.

Then, at the beginning of what would become a new era, a new sect emerged from Judaism which claimed the infinite God not only had created the world and given purpose to each of its parts, but had actually *entered* history as a human being, to show us how God intended us to live. Then for thirteen centuries, from the conversion of Emperor Constantine in 312 until the rise of Protestantism in the sixteenth century, the Christian Church with its theology and ritual, saints and feast days, shrines and crusades, supplied the background matrix—the myth—in which most of the European world found meaning and purpose. The rhythm of the liturgical year—Christmas to Easter to Pentecost, with all kinds of saints days between—gave a background against which a community or an individual could judge whether they synchronized with "the order of things."

The rhythm of "peak moments" of their family lives—birth, puberty, marriage, moments of moral failure, the death of loved ones—also found meaning in the sacraments, especially in the meal which celebrated their community and their inevitable triumph over suffering and death. All the segmented joys and sufferings of their lives somehow "fit" into a coherent, meaningful pattern. To all intents and purposes, just as for the pagan primitive, for thirteen centuries the sacred and the secular were one life.

Then in a gradual but cataclysmic conflict, the Reformation polarized God and Humanity between the radically other, flawless Divinity, on the one hand, and a radically corrupt humanity on the other. The reformers reduced religious expressions to the bare essentials, especially the sacraments. Only two remained: baptism and Eucharist, both purged of most of the otherworldly elements centuries had invested them with. Baptism now effected no inner change; the recipient remained a dunghill over which the merits of Christ were draped like concealing snow. The words of consecration effected no inner change in bread and wine; they were merely symbols, reminders of Christ's passion, death, and resurrection. Church art, which for centuries had been the illiterate peasants' Bible, was deemed idolatrous. The body of Christ was wrenched from the crucifix, stained glass windows were shattered, frescoes whitewashed, statues broken. All the physical symbols that supported a faith less rational than a theologian's faith disappeared.

The disenchantment of the world and human life had begun, not only within the new antagonistic religious denominations but outside as well. The rise of empirical science began to show clear, this-world explanations for phenomena preceding centuries had attributed to spirits and demons, to prayers answered or denied. The Enlightenment—a movement of purely rationalist philosophers in the eighteenth century—set about to emancipate the world from the tyrannical dominance of priests and bishops and to demythologize the hocus-pocus with which they enslaved the illiterate, to substitute the rational for the "irrational." Although the order of the universe convinced most of them there had to be an Ultimate Cause, an Architect, this Deity was too perfect to sully himself with the mundane matters of daily life. There was no need for—or effectiveness in—praying for divine intervention. There were now two totally separate worlds: the sacred and the secular, and rarely shall the twain meet.

These disenchanting ideas spread all over Europe and thence into their colonies. It culminated in the French Revolution in which kings and bishops went to the guillotine and, in a triumph of rationalism, a woman, the Goddess of Reason, danced naked on the high altar of the Cathedral of Notre Dame, before the shattered tabernacle.

Copernicus and Galileo had shown us we are not at the center of the universe—or even of this minor solar system. Later, Darwin offered evidence that we, the fine flower of civilization, were quite likely only slightly improved apes. Then Freud showed all the hopes and aspirations which keep us going are merely projections of the brute unconscious on a meaningless universe, and all our supposed sins are attributable to blind inner urges and events outside ourselves, neither of which we can control. We are not sinners, merely victims.

In the Industrial Revolution, utilitarianism ("What works?") made far more rational sense then "irrational" altruism ("What's right?"). Finally, Nietzsche liberated us from God altogether. Without a purposive Power to arbitrate moral disputes, there is only one arbiter: Might.

The practical Protestant work ethic became a kind of "civil religion," and Ben Franklin capsulized it in "God helps those that help themselves" (which many have quoted to me as coming from Scripture!). That devolved into the cynical advertising ploys of Phineas T. Barnum: "There's a sucker born every minute," and that dictum is still riding high in the boardrooms of Madison Avenue, on the Tube, billboards, slide-out postcards in every magazine. It is, in fact, a new "gospel": the American Dream, whose god is "the Economy."

Just as the gods gave meaning and a sense of coherence and purpose to the primitive, and Yahweh made sense out of life for the Hebrew, and Christ's message validated even suffering and death in Christendom, now the Economy serves those purposes. The priests of this myth are scientists, inventors, financiers, and advertisers, who answer our prayers for new things. We place a blinder faith than the primitive's in technology, gadgets, progress, and slavery to the electronic media. The soul of our society is not a spirit but a mass of electric circuits. In fact, the Economy, in a kind of *1984* Newspeak, has completely reversed the very meaning of the word. Before, it had always meant thrift, conserving, buying carefully, frugality. Now it means precisely the opposite: expansion, spending, monopoly. The bullish market has become the golden calf.

The moral code of the Economy is strict: work and compete. This is how you will find your true value: SATs, report cards, salaries, promotions, new car, designer jeans (which used to be poor people's pants). The Economy is celebrated in elaborate rituals: Super Bowls, Olympics, World Series, Oscars, Emmys, Tonys—which are not about sport or art but about money. Their practitioners make a hundred times the salary of the president of the United States. Rock concerts are liturgies of the Id. Shopping malls are cathedrals of consumption.

Once our hero was a farmboy named Lincoln, for whom the human appetite had a goal: human dignity. Now our hero is a farmboy named Presley, who "had it all" but killed himself. Yet years later, two thousand people still visit his shrine every day.

Functional Atheism

According to polls, few would confess outright to atheism. Yet judging from our society's accepted mores, a great many—even of those who profess theism—govern their behavior and choices by motives no different from those of the decent atheist down the block. "Church is church; business is business." It often seems, at least, that public worship rises from something other than a need to establish a person-to-Person connection with God (which is what the word "religion" means) but rather for peripheral reasons: "It's good for the kids. . . . The boss expects it. . . . What would our friends think if we didn't?" Given the question, "Will your being a Christian have any effect whatever on your choice of career?" about 80 percent say, "Of course not." The other 20 percent, who seem to respond positively, say, "Of course it will. I'm not going to be a pimp or a pusher or somebody like that"— as if being Christian meant only being un-bad.

We at least seem to live in a world without sinful or sacred. Confessions have certainly plummeted from the golden years of the forties and fifties (which is not a totally bad thing). But I have no few times finished hearing the confession of a fifteen-year-old boy and, just before giving him absolution, heard him say, "Oh, I sleep around a lot. That's not a sin, is it?" And this after what they themselves call eleven years of "Catholic brain-washing." Sixty to seventy percent say they routinely cheat on quizzes and tests; all but a few say, if they go to Mass, it's under protest; nearly all say they don't give their parents an honest day's work for an honest day's pay; about a third are sexually active and feel no compunction about it. I find most students genuinely believe themselves innocent until proven guilty—innocent even in their own eyes! Pretty ineffective brainwashing. The Electronic Baby-sitter has done a spectacularly better job.

If such people *genuinely* believed there is a God to whom they owe their very existence—and all the gifts that depended on that initial gift—if they claim they could never have known all the people they hold precious without the generosity of that Original Giver, surely that belief ought to be obvious in their lives and in their moral decisions. If they *genuinely* believed that, without this God, inevitable death would be not a transition but a total termination of their existence, surely this God would not be peripheral to their real lives. Perhaps my judgment is too harsh, but what they do shouts so loudly I can't hear what they claim.

A world without sacred or sinful, a world disenchanted, seems at first quite liberating. And yet there's something missing. We can feel very "big" in our unbothered, sanitized, forward-looking worlds. Until we look forward all the way. Like Lilliputians, we can become smug in our security, big shots, facing a rosy future no matter what we do today. Until Gulliver shows up. And in our case Gulliver is death.

In our society, death is both ignored and trivialized. On the one hand, death happens "somewhere else," in a nursing home or a hospital. Many of the seniors I teach have never been to a wake or funeral. On the other hand, children have seen more real deaths on the news and staged deaths on shows than a veteran in the army of Genghis Khan, to the point they can no longer tell the difference between the two. Death is unreal.

Oh, no. Death is the one reality in our future we can be sure of. It's the crucial reality. Death is inevitable, unpredictable, and—at least here—ultimate. No one gets out of here alive. Except for suicides, we have no idea when it will ambush us; I've presided at too many teenage funerals; nearly a hundred thousand Americans a year die by accident, "before their time." And death renders everything that went before it unchangeable.

There is an iron dichotomy: Either we go on (somehow), or we don't. No alternative.

Another iron dichotomy: Either God exists and offers us a chance to survive death, or God doesn't exist, and at death we simply stop being real. No alternative.

Either God exists right now—and is therefore very important, whether we like being indebted to God or not—or

God doesn't exist and never has, and we're out here swinging slowly, slowly in the wind, killing time before time kills us. We're all on the Titanic.

The God question isn't just academic, like "Are there intelligent beings on other planets?" The God question is really the *me* question: "Am I immortal, here and now? Or am I just so much potential garbage, and I don't know the collection date?"

After all the struggles, all the challenges, all the failures, to be wiped out like a computer file in a power outage? As Peggy Lee sang, "Is that all there is?"

With our blinders on, we seem to be so important, like the big shots in Lilliput. But in *Waiting for Godot*, Samuel Beckett captured the world without sinful or sacred, a world where God is nonexistent or at the very least irrelevant, a world from which we will never escape alive, a life in which eternity is a delusion. Beckett says, with a kind of whimsical gloom: "Astride of a grave and a difficult birth. Down in the hole, lingeringly, the gravedigger puts on the forceps."

Our lives seem leisurely and long, but from the objective viewpoint of the eight billion years the universe has been here, we're hardly a belch in a hurricane.

The Case Against Atheism

The French novelist and playwright Albert Camus claimed to be an atheist, but I have a hunch he was closer to an agnostic. In one of his novels a character says, "But what about God?" and another answers, "He doesn't exist, the bastard." The man sees that if there only were a God, no matter how unreadable his reasons for allowing unmerited human suffering, one could at least reassure oneself there *is* a reason. Camus also said that in the godless universe, the two greatest curses are intelligence and hope. Of all the species on earth, we are the only ones who can reason our way to the understanding that, ultimately, all our tragedies and triumphs are wiped out at death: Pfft! And yet, stupidly, we go on hoping.

This is one of my prime arguments *against* atheism. Undeniably, we do in fact have these two specifically human hungers: to understand and to survive death. But if in objective truth there are *no* answers, and if in objective truth we will *not* survive death, why are we the only species cursed—by our very human nature—with hungers for which no food exists? One would suspect that, according to the law of the survival of the fittest, only those who had divested themselves of intelligence and hope would survive. On the contrary, these two powers are precisely what keep us going!

Further, atheism seems to me—ironically—anti-intellectual, despite the fact that the only real atheists I've known or read were intellectuals. It seems at the very least unscientific to begin a quest (in this case for God) with an outright denial that the object of the quest *can* exist. To claim that would be as anti-intellectual as the papacy condemning Galileo because, despite his careful observations, the sun *can't* be in the center of the solar system, or, despite the wealth of evidence and legitimate inference to deny humans could have evolved from apes.

In the following chapter, we will examine the case for God, but until then let one argument suffice: Pascal's Wager. The French philosopher and mathematician Blaise Pascal said that at death there are clearly two—and only two—alternatives: Either we continue (somehow) or we don't. And there is not the slightest possibility here and now of determining with certainty which it is. One alternative is appealing; the other is appalling. Then if neither offers compelling evidence that it is the right one, I might as well take the appealing one! I live my life with the firm belief that it is only a running start for a better one, that everything does indeed have a purpose even though I can't yet discern it, that all the people who have been dealt awful hands by fate will somehow win. And if I'm wrong, Nietzsche is not going to be on the other side of death, thumbing his nose at me: "There, *Dummkopf!* I told you so!" Because he'll have evaporated, too.

If I'm wrong about God and my ultimate value, I'll never find out I was wrong!

Questions to Ponder and Discuss

✤ Suppose that in some new society being a true believer in God was a crime punishable by imprisonment. In all honesty, what *hard* evidence could the authorities bring in to court against you? Remember, no court could legitimately convict you on hazy notions that you feel and that others might have vague suspicions about. Nor could they convict you on occasional lapses into piety, like praying on the rare occasions when you're in a hole (like a foxhole). The evidence in your speech, actions, and choices would have to be consistent and serious.

✤ Before one ponders the evidence for God, it could be helpful—and honest—to give the opposition a fair chance. Role-play in your mind (or even write it out) an argument in which you take a resolutely atheist stance against an intelligent believer. Even if it goes against the grain, try as sincerely as you can to get into an atheist's mind and try to understand his or her considered motives for disbelief. If "two roads diverge in a yellow wood," and you are unaware the second road even exists, you don't take the other road freely—because it's the only road you know. Far from threatening a genuine belief in God, an honest assessment of atheism can strengthen it.

❧ Reread the paragraphs in which the text equates the American Dream and the Economy in our present society to a religion with priests, scriptures, symbolic rituals, saints. To your own mind, is the analogy justified or overdone? Accurate or simplistic? How deeply have narcissism, materialism, and utilitarianism permeated our society's values? How genuinely *free* are people—especially young people and those not used to thinking—to act against the "conventional wisdom"?

❧ Each of us feels comfortable at some place along the spectrum between the rational, left-brain approach to understanding at one end, and the intuitive, right-brain approach at the other end. Of course, as we have seen, in order to come to some kind of understanding of any reality, especially of God, we have to use both human powers. But do you personally tend to give greater weight to "the head" or to "the heart"? Is there a need to compensate to the other side?

❧ Judaism forbids any attempt to picture Yahweh lest it become an idol unto itself. Islam goes further and forbids any picture of any living thing, which is why mosques are decorated with geometrical patterns. Generally, Protestant churches are very sparely adorned, and recent Catholic church buildings seem equally "chaste." It might seem a small—and surface—point, but in your own dealings with God, do you find physical symbols a help or a hindrance? Are there any symbols that have a special meaning for you personally?

❧ Scripture: Acts 17:22-34; Job 27:7-10; 38:1-7

❧ *Catechism:* 2123-2141

The world is charged with the grandeur of God.
It will flame out, like shining from shook foil.
It gathers to a greatness, like the ooze of oil,
Crushed.

—Gerard Manley Hopkins, S.J., *God's Grandeur*

THE CASE FOR GOD

There are moments, rare but real, when we are ambushed by a sense of life, of the universal animatedness of everything, atoms carousing, neutrinos road-running through it all without hardly being slowed down. There's a suspicion of more, much more than we see or suspect. Even science agrees we have no direct experience of most of what's going on around us: rooms filled with unseen radio waves, most of the light spectrum that we can't see, the working within our own bodies, the true selves of even the people we love most. At privileged moments we stand looking up at the seemingly endless blaze of stars, tremble at the power of a stormy beach, sit in awe at an infant's tiny fist clasped around our pinkie finger. Those are moments when we helplessly say, "Oh, my God!" Which might be the quite proper response, the wordless awe which gives tribute to the Artist.

These are moments of ecstasy (*ekstasis*, standing outside), an invitation to go beyond the everyday, the pedestrian, the commonplace. At those times we experience the *numinous*, an elevating "presence" which is real but inexplicable. Strict rationalists claim such moments are delusions, self-induced, yet those who undergo them feel more like "victims" of this strange power than its fabricators. We're caught unaware by it, and no attempts to conjure it up seem to work. We *respond* rather than *impose*. Well, then, it's no more than the primitive response of the aborigine, which "gives" not only life but divinity to thunder, waterfalls, mountains, an atavistic throwback, like uneasiness passing a dark graveyard. Yet this yearning for the sacred is not a negative reaction of fear, but a desire for something quite positive: affirmation, enlivening, a connection with the Source of this energy we catch hints of. Like the intelligence and hope which so troubled Camus, why are we the only species that suffers from this hunger?

As Hamlet said to his friend, "There are more things in heaven and earth, Horatio, than are dreamt of in your philosophy." Or your science. Or your theology, for that matter.

This sense of the "holy," the "sacred," gets somewhat smeared by its association with "being untainted," virginal, morally unsullied. But the Greek, Semitic, and Latin meanings of "holy" go beyond morality to a real quality *within* the cause: the presence of the transcendent within our world, what Dietrich Bonhoeffer called "the Beyond in our midst." As we saw before, the experience of the *super*natural is not in the sense of physically above as in "superstructure," but rather an intensity of presence, as in superenergized." Thus, if one were living the supercharged life of God's grace, his or her life ought to be obviously more graceful and gracious.

Normally, when we use the words "religion" or "religious," we think of people who regularly attend a church, synagogue, or mosque. Such activities can indeed energize, uplift, supernaturalize our everyday lives, but they are not automatically efficacious, like dropping in to the mechanic's for a tune-up. A great many people who leave religious practice say, "I don't get anything out of it." (Which, when you think of it, is hardly what worship has always meant.) On the other hand, high-church worship can easily devolve into artistic performance and aesthetic response to it, and low-church worship can easily devolve into the moral challenge of the sermon and the feel-good jiving of the music. But the Latin root of "religion" is *religare*, *re-* meaning "again and again" or "back and forth," and *-ligare* meaning "to bind," as in "ligate." Thus, the radical meaning of religion is a strongly felt *connection* between the individual human soul (self) and God. Without that person-to-Person experience, there may be a great profusion of hymns and incense or a great deal of enthusiasm, but there is no genuine religion.

Mystery

Experience of the sacred is no more irrational than experience of loving sex is irrational. The two partners in a sexual act *know* when it is a true *connection* of souls or merely an interlocking of bodies. Just so, anyone at prayer or worship knows when this is truly a "joining" and when it is merely *pro forma* ritual. In both cases, this union is not merely a momentary surge of awareness but enlivening precisely because it is part of a full, lifetime *commitment* from both parties. Explaining simple orgasm to a ten-year-old, or explaining to sexually active teenagers the difference between casual and committed sexual union, or explaining a connection to the transcendent to anyone who has never experienced it, are all close to futile. One has to submit to it, vulnerably, to have even the remotest beginning of understanding. It's a mystery.

On the one hand, a mystery is not a problem—like a detective "mystery" or a question in math or the pieces of a jigsaw puzzle. The author doesn't know how the story is going to end; there is no set of answers in the back of the text; there are always pieces of the puzzle missing—in fact, there are pieces of other puzzles mixed in! On the other hand, a mystery is not some gnostic secret like voodoo, some blank darkness no human intelligence can penetrate. Rather, it is a question for which we will never find a boxed-in, final, certain, unarguably compelling, single answer. But we can venture into it, probe it, keep finding more and more. And more.

The question we began with is a mystery: "What the hell are human beings *for?*" We will never get a definitive answer to that one, but we can indeed keep finding more and more insights into it. In fact, one could make a very good case that probing that question more and more *is* what human beings *are* for! For all its clarity, science is a mystery, too, always open-ended, always reaching further, without the slightest hope of getting to "the End." Einstein said, "The most beautiful thing we can experience is the mysterious." Any human person is a mystery as well. You can accumulate the vital statistics, the family tree, the habits, the SATs, the Meyers-Briggs, thematic apperception results, credit ratings, and so forth, but you still have no more than a left-brain stereotype, perhaps a rough map to start out with. But the human person—self, soul, who-I-am—remains uniquely elusive. And love, surely, is a mystery. "Why have you spent fifty years with this woman rather than another?" Well, uh . . .

The only alternatives to making peace with mystery are the futile attempt to "solve" it or the impoverishing choice to ignore it altogether. Chesterton said poets don't go mad, chess players do; chess players try to cross the infinite sea (thus making it finite), which is by definition impossible and therefore frustrating; poets float on the infinite sea and enjoy its infinite mysteries. Spiritual "understanding" is not like other understandings. It doesn't deal with realities that can be objectified, captured, mastered, used—the way one might break and ride a mustang. On the contrary, if we are humble enough, it captures us, masters us, uses us.

The "solution" at the end of the book of Job is not a solution at all, at least not an answer to Job's rational craving for an intellectual justification for his agony. Rather, it is an answer to his soul, Person-to-person. Job doesn't "solve his problem" but rather "sees the light." The Presence which comes to him from the depths of the hurricane does not give an answer but is the answer, which Job doesn't possess but *experiences*. "In the past I knew only what others have told me. But now I have seen you with my own eyes." What Job understands at the end of his torment is the humbling, disturbing truth that if God exists, God is not answerable to us.

A mystery is always "beyond words," not because it can't be discerned but because one can begin to understand its inner truths only by going through a process—not just a routine rite but a vulnerable submission to a soul-experience. Siddhartha left his teachers because he learned that wisdom can't come through words but only through *contemplation*.

A Mind Behind It All

Nevertheless, faith in God is not a blind leap in the dark. Nor is it an assent compelled by evidence "so clear and distinct I can have no occasion to doubt it." Faith is a calculated risk. There is, at least to my mind, more than sufficient evidence that there must be a "Mind Behind It All." For the moment, that "Mind" is nonspecific. It does not limit itself to Yahweh, the Trinity, the Oversoul, Allah, or any other attempt by a particular creed to capture it. The only issue at the moment is whether there is an Entity outside our minds to *validate* the idea of a Supreme Being—which even atheists have.

Finally, because like human purpose, science, the unique person, and love, God is a mystery, the best one can hope for on the God question is a higher degree of *probability* that theism is the truth rather than atheism. Calculated risk. There is no other alternative; either a Higher Power exists or it does not. If that Power exists, all our denials will not make it go away; if that Power does not exist, the most profound belief will not make it real. One can only search the clues and decide which is the more probable answer. "Scientific proof" could offer no better.

The evidence for God is both notional and real. Notional knowledge is secondhand, academic, and probable—depending on the thoroughness of the research and honesty of the arguments. Most of what we accept as true is notional, garnered from personal reasoning and from the reliable, tested testimony of others. Real knowledge is firsthand, experiential, and certain. Seeing is not believing; seeing is knowing.

Notional Knowledge

Reason begins from evidence which is certain and works carefully toward conclusions which are probable. So I start with something I'm sure of: my intelligence. I know I have it. This intelligence tells me no effect can be greater than its causes. If I put a pumpkin on a table and it started to belt out "Hey, Big Spender," you'd have to surmise there was a speaker inside, because a pumpkin, all by itself, can't produce that effect without some help.

So apply this principle to my intelligence itself. Chemicals have power, but they don't seem able to change their minds; plants are adaptable, but I have no evidence that they *choose* to change; animals show shrewdness and trainability, but I don't expect even the smartest dog to write *Hamlet*, much less ponder its enigmas. None of those forebears seems capable of passing on whatever it is that gives me a speculative intelligence. Perhaps some space aliens came and zapped us into cognition. Whatever the source of intelligence, I know for sure it wasn't passed on by King Kong. The effect eludes a mindless cause. To deny a Mind Behind It All, I have to deny the very intelligence that asks the question.

Again, I apply the principle that no effect can be greater than its causes to the universe. It comes to me as a stunningly *ordered* piece of work. I don't impose the Periodic Table on the cosmos. Further, everywhere—according to the experts—the physical laws of nature are the same. Difficult to get "law" out of "luck," but that is what I'm stuck with if there is no ordering Mind. Every single object out there is doing the same thing: rotating on an axis and also revolving around another object, and that system revolves around another. Predictably. Having directed thirty some musicals, I find that particularly impressive, without a choreographer. I have no trouble with a big bang, but I do have difficulties with the unvarying predictability of its results. How do you get predictability from an accident? The effect eludes a mindless cause.

The theory of evolution, at least in its broader outlines, seems undeniable, too. But it seems (at least to me) to have a purposive plan. But if you use the word "plan," you're on the slippery slope to a mind. To speak of "natural selection" in a godless universe not only begs the question but is at the very least a misuse of words. Only a mind can see alternatives and *select* among them. Without a Mind Behind It All, "natural selection" is merely a description of what happened. In *Cosmos,* Carl Sagan wrote, "It is only by the most extraordinary coincidence that the cosmic slot machine has this time come up with a universe consistent with us." Indeed. If the earth was not tilted at 23 degrees, we would have no seasons; if its crust was ten feet thicker, there would be no atmosphere; if the moon was any closer, we would be inundated by tides twice a day. Among innumerable other fortunate accidents. To say that even life came about by sheer chance (much less intelligent life) would be equal to accepting that a hurricane could pass through an airplane junkyard and leave behind a working 747. The effect eludes a mindless cause.

Also, as we saw before, only humans have intelligence and hope, hunger to find reasons for the way things are and the desire to survive death. In a godless universe, though, there are no reasons, and we will all be annihilated at death. Why are we the only species cursed, by our very nature, with hungers for which there is no food? The effect eludes a mindless cause.

Testimony, as anyone who has watched a courtroom drama knows, is a much weaker support: people make inaccurate witnesses, are swayed by hidden agendas and prejudices, suppress focal evidence out of fear, etc. Perhaps the best testimony, then, is not the claims or words of the opposing views, atheism and theism, but the living testimony of their lives. Do they seem to "have a handle" on the question "What the hell are people for?"

I have read many atheists, and some seem to me surprisingly noble; Albert Camus is one shining example. But most seem, for all their jigs and japes, a very honest but very gloomy lot; Samuel Beckett and Jean Genet come to mind. And well they might be dour, when their most profound belief is that human life is absurd and everything ultimately futile—even their writing. Conversely, however, many of my fellow believers are stupefyingly rigid, puritan, small-minded, vindictive, tight-fisted, juiceless, and joyless. I sense in the Grand Inquisitors and Ayatollahs none of the energy, the superhumanizing effect that must come from an authentic "connection" to a transcendent, liberating Power. There is no power in them but *their* power. They seem to be not models of the connection but perversions of it: self-connected.

On the other hand, I do sense such a connection in the lives of Dag Hammarskjold, Pearl Bailey, Thomas More, Einstein, Dorothy Day, Gandhi, Schweitzer, Golda Meir. They could have passed Clair Booth Luce's test: You can see their freedom; you can feel their joy. All I know is that, if all those radiant people were stupid to believe, I want to be stupid with them.

Real Knowledge

Atheists say that, unlike experiments to validate the presence of unseen atoms, there are no experiments to validate the presence of an unseen Deity. Theists disagree. They insist we can engage in an experiment: praying—not "saying prayers" or engaging in liturgical worship, but opening ourselves with as complete vulnerability as possible and allowing our souls to be manipulated by the Beyond in our midst. (For more, see the final chapter.)

I can speak only of my own personal, firsthand experience; for me, everyone else's experience of God is secondhand testimony. Probably the most profound encounter was in the year before I was to be ordained. All my life I'd predicated my value as a human being on my grades, and for six years studying Thomistic metaphysics (in Latin) my grades were several rungs below mediocrity. I was despondent, virtually ready to kill myself, nearly certain I was incompetent to be a priest. Then one afternoon alone in my room, I lay down and tried to get away from it. Suddenly, I was—literally—taken out of myself. I was unaware of the room or time passing. And I *knew* I was in the presence of God. It was like drowning in light. And I knew, as certainly as I knew I was alive, that I was accepted. That I was a good man, and I'd be a good priest, and I never had to prove it to anyone else again.

I had—beyond the need or possibility of proof—encountered God. All the head-trip stuff, all the theology, was no more than the first stage of a rocket, like the research you do before interviewing someone. Once you've met God himself, there's no longer need for proof.

That happened in 1963. It's worked for thirty-seven years, 13,500 days of work, love, anger, trust, frustration, joy, betrayal, triumph, failure. And I feel about God as one lifelong spouse feels about another: "I'd rather be unhappy with you than happy without you." And as Pascal said, if I'm wrong, I'll never find out I was.

Science says there can be no reality faster than light. Yet science also delights in playing "what if." Well, what if there *were* a light, an energy, faster than light? It would be moving so fast it would be everywhere at once. Like God. So dynamic it would also be utterly at rest. Like God. And science now believes when it cracks open the last building block of matter it will find non-extended energy. Like God. $E=mc^2$ means matter is energy. There is an insight there.

Couple that modern insight with the insight of Exodus. When Moses asked Yahweh his name, he was asking for much more than a label. For a Hebrew, one's name designated his or her role in the community. And God's reply was "I am who am." What is God's role in the community? Existence. God is the pool of existence out of which anything that is gets its "is." At least in this sense, insofar as the power of God is immanent, God is the *anima mundi,* the soul of the world! When we react in awe and reverence to the numinous in nature, we are reacting to the Source of its aliveness and energy: "The world is charged with the grandeur of God."

Questions to Ponder and Discuss

✸ Describe a situation where you yourself have had a sense of the numinous, the sacred emanating from nature or art or people. How would you defend this experience as an encounter with something truly "there," as opposed to a mere feeling into which you invested more importance than was really present?

✸ "There are more things in heaven and earth, Horatio, than are dreamt of in your philosophy." List for yourself the "things" you are certain are true but for which you could offer no convincing evidence to someone skeptical about such "things." (This is not unlike the first question: What are you really sure of?)

✸ Big one. When you pray, when you try to contact God, how does it *feel?* Do you have the sense this is a person-to-Person communication—even if there are no words, no revelations, nothing to write down as a "product"? Do you feel a connection with another personal Being who, although he/she doesn't speak, is sincerely listening? If praying is just "saying prayers," keeping up a contact like an e-mail to which no one responds, from which you garner no sense of being listened to, can you assess why? What are the obstacles within yourself to simply "letting go" and letting God "ravish" you? Somehow Our Lady found it at the annunciation: "Be it done unto me according to your word." How could meditating on her posture before God help you to get out of God's way in allowing him to take hold of your soul?

✤ Reversing a question in the last chapter: Imagine you are in an argument with an honest, intelligent atheist. How would you justify your belief in God—not with assertions of faith ("Of course God exists, how else could all this stuff have gotten here! Of course God exists. He sent his only-begotten Son to save us from our sins.") Use arguments in defense of God which an honest atheist would at least have to chew over.

✤ Have you ever felt a time in your life when God was really touching you? We're not talking here just of a sense of the numinous presence of "something other." We're talking about a sense you really were in *connection* with a Person who is the Beyond in Our Midst. Beware of times when your grandmother was saved from cancer or you escaped death in an accident. That could have been just coincidence and luck. Hold yourself to a time or times when you *knew* Someone was *there*.

✤ Relax somewhere. Put this book away. Just sit there, utterly still, receptive, and try to list in your mind all the things and activities in that room which surely are "going on" but of which you are completely unaware, things you know *must* be occurring but of which you have no direct experience. Somewhere among those activities, I'm betting God is lurking.

✤ Scripture: Psalm 139; Job 10:11-13; Matthew 10:28-31; 23:36-38

✤ *Catechism:* 33, 35, 218-221, 271, 302-314, 370,1718

If I take the wings of morning and settle at the farthest limits of the sea, even there your hand shall lead me, and your right hand hold me fast.

—Psalm 139:9-10

✳ 6 ✢

THE OTHER FACES OF GOD: WORLD RELIGIONS

There is a story of a group of blind people taken for a stroll in a park in Calcutta. Somehow, their guide disappeared, and they were left to paw their way around, trying to find help. One shouted, "Oh, I found a wall! Maybe there's a gate." Another felt around her feet and said, "No. We're still lost. I can feel the tree stumps." Yet another reached up and said, "You're right. I can feel the big palm leaves." A fourth cried, "Ah! There's a snake in that tree!" Still another cried out, too, "Oh! A spear! Are you a guard? Can you help us?" The final blind man reached up and said, "I found a rope. Maybe it's a bell. Oh, it smells really bad."

What they had found, of course, was an elephant. Their isolated perceptions of the same object were far from the reality. Even lumped together, they add up to a pretty bizarre picture—but nonetheless better than any one of them alone. The same is true with God. Each of our understandings of the Mind Behind It All can be enriched if we shout across our doctrinal and denominational walls, "What does God look like from where you stand?"

At least to my individual (lifelong Western, rational, Christian) mind, the pictures of God I see from many other world religions rest uncomfortably with my personal experience of God. Some views (pantheism, polytheism, paganism) seem to make God too *immanent,* this-worldly, locked into creation, when my reasoning tells me the Creator of the universe must be unspeakably beyond anything material and changeable. Other apprehensions of God (deism, Islam, most forms of Eastern religion) seem to make God too transcendent, otherworldly, aloof from creation, when my experience tells me I can sense God lurking under the skins of everything I touch. Still, each viewpoint acts as a corrective when my own perception of God becomes unbalanced. When I start getting too head-trip, theologizing, the immanent view reminds me God is not only the Uncaused First Cause but my Friend; when I lean to the other side, dealing with God as "Jesus, he's mah ol' Buddy!" transcendent religions remind me God is also unspeakably Other.

Beyond the large-picture conceptions each religion has, some specific doctrines also make me uncomfortable, not just about weird practices like snake handling and whirling dervishes, but attitudes about human behavior. I'm ill at ease with what at least seems an extreme concern of Eastern religions for the sacredness of all life, to the point sacred cows roam the streets of India while the people they pass by are starving. I'm reluctant to accept the Muslim belief in Jihad or (perhaps more tellingly) their abhorrence of even moderate use of alcohol.

However, in what follows, I will try to avoid such antagonisms and concentrate rather on insights into God from other world religions which seem fruitful for consideration by any honest seeker after the Mind Behind It All. We have faced the first question: Is there a God? Now to the second question: What is God like? What kind of entity is God? What is God's "personality"—the things God likes and dislikes, the divine purposes we can discern from the world God made? "What does God look like from where you stand?"

All religions grow out of a sacramental experience of the holy in the here-and-now. In both East and West, they began with personifications of that felt power in anthropomorphic gods but, with time, reflection and sophistication, a more rarefied single Deity emerges. The Western mind has been profoundly influenced by the clear-minded Greeks, intolerant of fuzzy ideas and the ambiguity of complementarity. On the contrary, like practitioners of modern science, the Eastern mind is quite comfortable with ambiguity, paradox, and what a Westerner would see as outright contradictions. The Western believer could learn a great deal from the Eastern believer.

Hinduism

The essence of Hinduism, the oldest of the Eastern religions, is *oneness*. There is no word for "religion" in Hindi since, unlike Western religions, the transcendent "connection" is not compartmentalized into one time in the week or a particular sacred space, but pervades every crevice and corner of life. Every object, person, and place is saturated with the sacred.

The Ultimate Reality—Brahman ("ever growing")—is a neuter noun, not a proper name. At least in early Hindu writings, God is incapable of deliberate action, therefore not a person but the essence of the world-soul in all beings. Here's where a tolerance for ambiguity becomes important. The Brahman is one and many, becoming and unchanging, personal and impersonal, fullness and emptiness, good and evil. The Hindu God is, in fact, *beyond* all predicates, even beyond "is." This does not mean God "is not" but that the mode of God's existence is so far beyond what we mean in any other use of "to be" that applying it to God would be close to blasphemous in its diminishment. Unlike the God of the West, the Brahman is not a lawgiver. It is also beyond good and evil. Prayer is not person-to-Person but, to indulge a crude analogy, more like connection to a transcendent Generator of Life Energy.

The Atman (again, neuter) is the presence of the Brahman—the immortal soul—within the individual. The world-soul and the self-soul are one. "Atman *is* Brahman" is not unlike science's "Matter *is* energy," or like the statement of Jesus, "I and the Father are one." The very essence of Hinduism is realizing that oneness.

One of the key terms in Hindu beliefs is *samsara*, repeated rebirths into a new more (or less) purified life, thus the notion of *caste*, each reincarnation raising or lowering one's status in the overall scheme of things. One's direction at rebirth is governed by *karma*, the state of one's moral and spiritual life at each death. Violate the underlying order of the universe, and you will pay the price in your next life—not by the judgment of God but because that's the way things are. The moral code is *dharma*: righteousness, duty, honesty, decency, respect, and care for others. But as one rises the ladder of castes, the demands for a purer dharma increase.

Becoming part of the Oneness is not to be *saved* but to be *liberated*, from the everyday self, which is maya, usually misleadingly translated "illusion." Actually, the workaday world is real, but only in the sense dreams are real. Compare that to modern science's belief that the chair which supports your whole weight is nonetheless not *really* solid at all, but a carousel of moving parts—and most of it is empty space. Reality is relative to your ability to perceive it. When one has come to an acceptance of life's illusions, he or she is ready for the path of renunciation. *"Yoga"* comes from the same Indo-European root as the word "yoke," simultaneously uniting and controlling, pointing toward integrating the Atman with the Brahman, and the methods of yoga are most adaptable to individual temperaments: yogas for those who are more reflective, or affectionate, or active, or contemplative.

Hindus can teach us much about God and our connection to God, especially that, compared to children, we are adults, but compared to saints, we are children.

Buddhism

Buddhism is a kind of Hindu "protestantism," which began in reaction against Hindu excesses: exploitative castes, nit-picking speculation, mystery degraded into superstition. To counteract these, in about 570 B.C. the Buddha (a title, not a proper name: "The Awakened") evolved a worldview and system of self-discipline with no authorities or castes, no elaborate ritual, no speculative theology but rather focus on one's own soul, no shackling traditions, no salvation from outside one's own sovereign self. Buddha neither accepted nor rejected a personal God, which puzzles Western minds. God is not creator, listener, helper. Buddhism is a very much do-it-yourself religion and, as with Hinduism, offers a "connection" which is not personal. Hindus picture the individual soul as a mango pit wrapped in leaves, and when you unwrap the final leaf, there is the pit: the soul; but Buddhists see the soul as an onion, and when you pull back the final leaf there is . . . nothing. Unsettling, but again it is like modern science which says that, when you crack open the most basic atomic particle, you will find . . . nonextended energy.

Buddha found that the essence of human life is to suffer in a transitory world in which the greatest fear is not death but rebirth into yet another grinding confrontation with suffering. He saw that theological speculation does nothing at all to relieve all-consuming suffering, so he offered an explanation of the causes of suffering and a practical program to cure it. The cause of suffering is selfish desire, and the end of suffering comes from release from the narrow limits of self-interest through eight ways of living "rightly": right knowledge, aspirations, speech, behavior, livelihood, effort, mindfulness, absorption. At the core of it all is *concentration* which focuses the self and sloughs off all its impurities. The result is attainment of *Nirvana*.

Nirvana is another puzzling idea. Its root means "to extinguish," which suggests that achievement of fulfillment is a sort of "soul-suicide" and that Buddhism is basically an atheist humanism. In a wrongful analogy: The individual soul has a separate identity like a single droplet of water but, through gradual purgation, it is finally absorbed into the Oversoul, like the droplet engulfed by the ocean—thus losing its identity. However, Nirvana is *not* annihilation but bliss, and if there is bliss there must be a *subject* to experience it. Invoking complementarity again: Nirvana is *both* absorption *and* separateness, bliss uncontaminated by either attachment or dependence. The best explanation I have found is that it is not the droplet which is absorbed by the ocean, but the droplet absorbs the ocean! [Judge which end of the left-lobe/right-lobe spectrum you lean toward by trying to digest that statement!]

The usual statues of the Buddha and the crucifix distill the essence of the two beliefs and give a rough idea of their contrasts. Buddha is usually seated in a lotus position, eyes closed, focused in self-enclosed concentration. Jesus on the cross is most often wide-eyed, mouth gaping, reaching his arms wide to the world. Christianity reaches for a connection between two discrete persons; Buddhism reaches inward to the source of essential power. The great Christian mystics opened their souls blissfully that God might enter and ravish them; the Buddhist mystics close round their own essence and blind themselves to all else but the God already within.

One wonders if Francis of Assisi and Therese of Lisieux, Teilhard de Chardin and Albert Einstein might find much to share with the Buddha.

Taoism

Used strictly, the word "religion" hardly pertains to Taoism, whose adherents who do engage in ritual cult (very few) usually limit themselves to what other religions would consider superstition: mediums, shamans, exorcists, spells. More important to someone exploring God from a Christian perspective is Taoism's *attitude*. Its basic insight is to *yield* to the Tao (the Way things really are) openly, freely, easily, adaptively, serenely confident. Go with the flow, submit to the Tao rather than trying to dominate it or manipulate it with unheard prayers.

That yielding, as we saw when we first considered complementarity, is symbolized in the endless fluctuations back and forth of the feminine Yin and the masculine Yang—a circle bisected by a wavy line, one side white, the other black, but each with a spot of the other color within it. It is a perfect whole, fluctuating yet balanced. No one can tell whether it is a white circle with a black half or vice versa. It is a synthesis of rest and movement.

Taoism is a bipolar relationship of all the opposites in our lives—masculine/feminine, rational/intuitive, aggressive/submissive, beast/angel, autonomy/community, sacred/secular, justice/ mercy, etc. The form of one side of the circle gives form to the other but always gradually balances out. The clearest image it offers about our attitude is to be "humble as water," which yields to the storm and to the calm. "Bide in silence, and the radiance of the spirit shall come in and make its home."

But neither yielding nor silence are too popular in our present ethos. Alas.

Judaism

All three of the major Western religions are joined in Judaism at their roots. The Jews' "way of looking at" the relationship between the transcendent/immanent Presence and our human relationships with "him" tinges whatever later developments each of these great traditions made by branching off from the common Source. God is the Unique One, and all else in the universe are his creations, subservient and beholden to him. One sentence captures the heart of Judaism, which a fervent Jew says every day and which is tacked to their doorposts in a *mezuzah*, the Shema: "Hear, O Israel, the Lord our God, the Lord is One."

Judaism is an ethical monotheism—a single God has written his law into all things. Unlike the religions of the East, there might be room for angels and saints, but no other gods, however minor and dependent. Also unlike most Eastern beliefs, the God of Israel and its two major offshoots is a clearly *personal* Deity who carries on a loving relationship with his people and, in the case of Israel, enters into a unique Covenant with them which can be understood only by analogy to a marriage. Most of our simplistic images of the God of the Hebrew Scriptures come not from the Bible (the most bought and least read book in history), but from art and movies, particularly Cecil B. DeMille's *The Ten Commandments:* a scowling, bearded old man filled with vengeance and threats—which was not God at all, but Moses!

And it was not Moses either, but Charlton Heston, whose personality was not at all like the biblical Moses. The Moses of Exodus was far more like Don Knotts! Most often the Bible shows Yahweh as a loving husband, betrayed by his beloved Israel for false gods, yearning for her return.

No Eastern religion has any real concern for history, but for the Jews their history is their identity. "To be" *means* "to be with"—united to Yahweh, to the People, and to the Book. They are sons and daughters of Abraham and Sarah; their family tree includes Isaac, Jacob, Joseph, Moses, David, Solomon, Ruth, the long line of prophets like Isaiah and Jeremiah, the warlike Maccabees, all of whose lives are treasured in the Book and whose tragedies and triumphs they celebrate yearly.

The Jewish scriptures are a very diverse record of God's self-manifestations, a library of laws, poems, stories, history, wisdom. The Law *(Torah)* is, strictly speaking, the Pentateuch, the first five books: Genesis, Exodus, Leviticus, Numbers, and Deuteronomy, which offer not only the stories of their origins in the twelve sons of Jacob (whose name was changed to *Israel,* "he who wrestles with God"), but the formation of the people in the Exodus from Egypt, as well as the principles by which to judge new problems not envisioned by the original sages.

There is no official, normative list of core beliefs in Judaism, like the Apostles' Creed in Christianity. The closest is the simple statement of the Shema. That unique God is in no way like the icy rationalist distillation of the Greeks, nor like the rarefied, elusive, and unforthcoming Ultimate of the Eastern religions. Unlike those beliefs, Yahweh is not at all beyond moral goodness. Rather, moral uprightness is constitutive of who Yahweh is.

God is holy, complete unto himself, unapproachable, utterly transcendent, and yet he is also *present*, his house at the center of the Jewish capital: *Emanuel,* "God with us." God is the creator; everything depends on him not only for its existence but its purposes. God is particularly partial to the downtrodden: the poor, the widow, the orphan, the foreigner. God intrudes unbidden, choosing the least likely in the community to go on daunting missions. God delegates authority—stewardship—over his creation to his people. God promises not only to be with his People but to send a hero, a messiah, to inaugurate a new age.

The Sabbath commemorates the day the Lord rested at the end of creation, separated clearly from the rest of the secular week. It is not merely a negative abstention from physical labor but also a positive invitation to meditate on the truths of the Book and the traditions of the People. Throughout the year, the rhythm of Jews' months resonates to the rhythm of their history, remembering at Passover their liberation from slavery, at Rosh Hashanah and Yom Kippur their need for penance and forgiveness.

The idea of "the Chosen People" often looks to outsiders like some kind of dismissively exclusive, even smugly condescending attitude. Nothing could be further from the truth. Israel is not Yahweh's pampered pet, but rather his messenger, yoked to the intimidating task of being God's model of moral uprightness to the nations, and more often than not also God's scapegoat, the Suffering Servant who bears the burden of all peoples' guilt and agony.

It is astonishing how much this Chosen People, who now amount to little more than 2 percent of humanity, have contributed to the wider civilization, far beyond their proportions. We owe our weekend to the Jews (and God bless them for it). But for such a numerically tiny group, they seem inordinately blessed with a love for learning, a passion for justice, a heroic sense of endurance, and a creativity unmatched by any other single ethnic body: Sigmund Freud, Karl Marx, Albert Einstein, Benjamin Disraeli, Mark Chagall, Leonard Bernstein, Mortimer Adler, Jonas Salk—not to mention uncountable statesmen, actors, entertainers, novelists, philosophers.

Islam

Rather than a catalogue of beliefs, Islam is a core conviction which a Muslim recites five times a day: "There is no God but Allah, and Mohammed is his prophet." The very word "Islam" means "submission, resignation," the unwavering surrender in faith shown by our common father, Abraham, whose firstborn son, Ishmael, is the root of the Arab nations. Unlike the complexities of Eastern religions, Islam is as stark, uncluttered, and intense as the desert from which it emerged. And like Judaism and medieval Christendom, Islam is not simply a religion but a whole *culture*.

At the age of forty-one, praying in a cave on Mt. Hira above the city of Mecca, Mohammed was overwhelmed by a vision— just as Abraham, Moses, Samuel, Jeremiah, and Jesus: "You are the one." He was filled with the conviction he had been chosen by the one God to bring his people back to him. At first, Mohammed was ravaged by anguish and doubts. Was this a self-deception or even the work of the Evil One? For a year or two, the visions failed him, and he began to doubt this vocation. But his wife, Khadijah, believed in him, and slowly he began to share his understanding of Allah with young people, the poor, and slaves.

For twenty-three years he preached the one God in the face of innumerable pagan gods, receiving the same scornful response the Hebrew prophets had suffered. So finally, on July 16, 622 A.D., Mohammed set off with about forty followers to the city of Medina. It was the day of the *Hejira*, from which Muslims would forever date their calendars, for his journey resulted in almost uninterrupted successes, culminating eight years later in his return to Mecca. Mohammed fused together all the bickering tribes into the Covenant of Medina, the first leader in history to guarantee religious freedom to all creeds.

From all reports, Mohammed himself was humble, affectionate, charming, thoughtful, and utterly impartial, yet he transformed into a statesman who forged a religious community with its own structure of laws and institutions that has lasted thirteen hundred years. Even so, he scorned palaces, milked his own goats and mended his own clothes, like the Hindu Mohandas Gandhi.

He died in 632, with almost all of Arabia under his mastery. At its height, Islam controlled the northern half of Africa, all of the Near East, Afghanistan, Pakistan, and Indonesia, and assimilated to its language and religion more than the Greeks ever had. Today, five hundred million all over the world follow his beliefs and daily revere his name.

The Koran *(Qur an)*, the Islamic scripture, is the one book in which there is no doubt. It is the very word of God dictated to Mohammed by the angel Gabriel, written by scribes as Mohammed recited it in an ecstatic state. Mohammed was not the only prophet, but he was the last, the "seal" of the prophets, of whom twenty-eight are mentioned in the Koran, including eighteen from the Hebrew scriptures as well as John the Baptist and Jesus.

Allah is unique and incomparable, beyond even the weak reaches of speculative theology or poetic analogy. Mohammed accepted Jesus as a prophet but not as divine, and in contrast to the strong immanence of God in both Jewish and Christian views, Allah is utterly transcendent, in his being much more like the Ultimate Reality of Eastern beliefs. Thus, prayer for the Muslim is a one-way conversation. Allah is creator, ruler, judge, and all that is depends on him.

To whom is Allah merciful? To those who submit unquestioningly to his will. (Therefore, orthodox Islam is not open to much social change like the liberation of women.) Mohammed evolved the Golden rule into definite law, which is the Five Pillars of Islam. (1) The simple creed: "There is no God but Allah, and Mohammed is his prophet." (2) Prayer five times a day to keep one's life in perspective. (3) Charity: Two and a half percent of one's holdings (not just income) every year to the poor. (4) Penance: During the month of Ramadan, abstinence from food and drink from sunrise to sundown in order to understand the plight of the poor. (5) Pilgrimage: Once in a lifetime each Muslim must travel, all in the same simple clothes, to Mecca.

It is almost unthinkable that any but the most ardent Christians would pause to pray five times a day, abstain for an entire month, and surrender two and a half percent of all holdings each year for the poor. Recent attacks by fanatic Muslim tarnish the true Islam just as the Crusades tarnished the true Christianity.

Both Sides Now

[To lessen the basic discrepancy between the East's seemingly impersonal and the West's surely personal Ultimate Reality, in this concluding segment, I will use the pronoun "It."]

When we look at the religions of the world, we find all kinds of people talking about the same elephant, in different dialects of the same language. Each contains some version of the Golden Rule; each sees self-centeredness as the root of our troubles; each acknowledges a universal Source from which we have sprung and in relation to which our true fulfillment (salvation) is to be found. Each shows a willingness to sacrifice any finite concern which comes in conflict with union with that ultimate, transcendent Truth. "God lets his rain fall on the just and the unjust." Surely then, he would let his light fall on other genuine believers as well.

Existence. All of the major religions agree that the Divine exists and is utterly unique. Morever, at the very least, whatever the Ultimate is, it is to some degree knowable, and yet by definition confoundingly elusive of capture in human terms. It is "like" other entities only in the remotest way. All agree that the Sacred is real and substantive, although they differ in the ways and degrees in which it is "real."

Connection. Whether we acknowledge it or not, there is an onto-logical (objectively existent) "connection" between the Ultimate and humankind. Without Its existence, our existence would be meaningless. And there is a reciprocal relationship between It and us, but it is the *nature* of that relationship which undergirds the differences between West and East. The three religions rooted in Abraham see the Ultimate as our efficient cause (the Creator), our formal cause (the Ruler), and our final cause (the Exemplar and Goal); the Oriental religions see It as the absolutely pure being, in contrast to which our "being" is illusory.

All religions agree that the Entity on the other side of the abyss is good, benevolent, and, at least in some sense, supportive, despite variously viewed "powers of evil." All agree that our response should be at the very least respectful and at best an attempt to conjoin ourselves with It through prayer and/or worship. This connection is as mysterious as a long-term loving relationship between two human beings, and yet it is not the human give-and-take relation-ship but rather a yielding to undeserved love, i.e., grace.

Moral Behavior. All the great religions agree that, given the nature of our relationship with the Ultimate, we ought to order and structure our this-world lives in accordance with the super-natural Reality which gives them a framework of meaning. The will of the Ultimate, manifest in "the way things are," shows us a structure of natural laws which indicate what elements of our lives are life-giving or death-dealing to an immanent-transcen-dent union. In the face of that relationship, "value" takes on a meaning far more potent and real than price tags.

Revelation. In the East, the Source is impersonal and almost beyond the concept of abstraction—yet it is in some degree detectable and knowable. For them, as Ward Fellows (to whom I am much indebted) puts it with admirable conciseness, revelation is really a "To Whom It May Concern" letter. In contrast, the West sees revelation as truly interpersonal, either to the community through a prophet or Person-to-person within an individual soul, from a *caring* God.

Salvation. All the major religions agree that human beings are in need of "salvation." All believe that something within us restrains us from the greatness toward which some other movement within us impels us. They all agree that there are realities in our lives that lead to spiritual death and realities that lead to more profound and abundant spiritual life.

The goal of salvation in the East is release from contentment with inferior reality, from a complacent failure to actuate one's own divine potential. In the West, the soul-sickness is willful refusal to yield center stage to the Creator; salvation heals our estrangement from the true order of things which *is* God's will. In the East, there is no sense of collective salvation, while community is a staple of the Western notion: a Chosen People, the Kingdom of God, Islamic theocracy.

One of the strongest divergences is in the *means* to salvation. In the East, it is very much a bootstrap operation, individualistic, without any help from Above. By contrast, in the West, although we must cooperate with the Divinity, in the end salvation comes as a free gift from God. Again, this is perhaps clearest in the two greatest exemplars of East and West, the Buddha and Jesus Christ. The Buddha took hold of himself, struggled might and main to find the clearest route to fulfillment, and ground away at it until he broke free. In contrast, the Jesus we see on the cross is the epitome of helpless surrender who conquered by sheer impotence.

In the end, all religions agree: There is something profoundly wrong with us, and our mission from the Ultimate is to right that wrong. But all of them are also in agreement—and offer multitudinous evidence—that the estrangement can, indeed, be healed.

Questions to Ponder and Discuss

❧ Many of us who are older remember a time when giving another religion even some measure of respect was hardly thinkable, much less trying to understand that faith from the point of view of its (otherwise obviously intelligent) adherents. Hindus, Buddhists, Taoists, Jews, and Muslim were, well . . . strange, with their outlandish customs, clothing, practices. On the other hand, we ourselves held "the one true faith," and our customs were tried and true and therefore "normal." There was a firm belief, in perhaps the majority, that "outside the Church there is no salvation," and "salvation" meant avoiding a literal, fiery, eternal hell some time in the future, and "Church" meant exclusively the Roman Catholic Church. Even since before Vatican II, however, that exclusivity was becoming somewhat embarrassing, insular, snobbish. Do you personally feel reluctant to probe into quite different approaches to the same God? Is it just "too much at once"? Would you be more comfortable trying for a while to establish your own personal "connection" with God and then coming back to others' views to fine-tune it?

❧ Reflect on the Hindus' basic belief in the oneness of all that is. Everything we see—and all the realities that are there but we don't see—shares existence, holds within it a spark of the divine life of God who told the Hebrew Moses his very *name* was "Existence." Pantheism says that everything *is* God, which automatically denies that God is the creator, since the creator would have to preexist his creation and therefore be independent of it. But wariness about pantheism can deny us a very real insight into God and a real sense of God's immanent presence. God is not his creation, but God is *in* his creation—and in every tiniest facet of it. Think back to the "What if" section of the last chapter and the nonextended energy at the heart of the smallest subatomic particle, the world "charged with the grandeur of God." Retire into your innermost soul, your *Atman*. Can you feel that Presence, at the very core even of yourself? If not, what could be holding back your yielding to it?

✤ Near the end of his life, Thomas Aquinas said that, compared to the reality of God, all that he had ever written (and he had written encyclopedically!) was "straw." If perhaps the greatest of all Catholic theologians would say that even his meticulous, penetrating intelligence and saintly spirit could not capture the essence of God, what of us poor ordinary minds? Is it ultimately futile even to try? Yet if God is the ultimate source of all, the one who gives us our very existence and purpose, could anyone of honest mind *not* try to understand God just a little bit more richly than we did last year or the year before?

✤ The Jews gave us Jesus. And Jesus had been imbued from his childhood with all that Judaism meant; the New Testament depends for its credibility in great part as fulfilling what had always been called the Old Testament, the Hebrew Scriptures. It may seem merely an academic exercise, but it could be enlightening to ponder first what Christianity took over whole from Judaism (the Sabbath, a meal celebrating liberation, atonement of sins) and then in what ways it went beyond Judaism (the divinity of Christ, the incarnation, the resurrection).

✤ Every philosopher from Buddha to Karl Marx began with suffering. Why? It seems self-evident that human beings were born to seek happiness. But what does happiness really mean? It can't be being unbothered, "unsuffering"; if that were true, the most fulfilled human would be a drunkard—or dead. It can't be money-fame-sex-power; too many people have had those to the max and yet felt unfulfilled. Whatever happiness—human fulfillment—means, it has to factor being at peace with inevitable suffering into the formula. Why?

✤ Scripture: Acts 17:22-34

✤ *Catechism:* 839-848

Though he was in the form of God, he did not regard equality with God as something to be exploited, but emptied himself, taking the form of a slave.

—Philippians 2:6-7

❋ 7 ❋

YOUR BASIC CHRISTIAN

As we saw in the Introduction, too often those in charge of instructing those interested in the Catholic faith presume conversion before the process starts and skip right on to outlining the principles of the faith (catechesis), which is like English teachers who want to jump right into the stories they like to teach rather than bothering with basic syntax and outlining. Moreover, Catholic catechesis concentrates too much and too soon on what *divides* Catholics from other Christians rather than first explaining what nearly all believing Christians would accept about Jesus' life and message. This, in turn, is like teaching calculus before teaching basic math. The Christian denominations differ, for instance, on the way in which Christ is present at the Eucharist and when and how this presence occurs. If the Reformers and Counter-Reformers could have sat down and agreed that Christ is *somehow* more intensely present during the Eucharist than anywhere else, without trying to box it into the perfect formula, we might all still be worshiping together. As Will Rogers said, "If preachers would concentrate more on our Savior's message and less on how he arrived here and departed, we'd all be a lot better off."

Therefore, this chapter will focus on Your Basic Christian, what most Christians—by and large, more or less, on the whole, generally, broadly speaking—would agree to about Christ and being Christian, without getting too picky about it. That can wait for later. And not much then.

Christianity was founded not on theory but on experience of a composite event: the life, death, and resurrection of Jesus Christ. Christianity's claim to credibility rests on several not compellingly certain truths: the reliability of the gospel sources, the divinity of Christ, and most especially Jesus' resurrection. As Saint Paul wrote, "If Christ has not been raised from death, then we have nothing to preach and you have nothing to believe" (I Corinthians 15:14).

If any one of those foundations is false, there is no need to read another line.

Reliability of the Gospels

Almost the sole sources of evidence about the life, teaching, death, and resurrection of Jesus are the four gospels of Mark, Matthew, Luke, and John—and they were hardly unbiased reporters. On the contrary, they were men whose whole lives had been transformed by their belief that the protagonist of their stories was, in fact, the incarnation of the one God. Therefore, they did not describe events with the same eyes as people who were on the spot when they occurred. Rather, they pictured the

events as they believed them *really* to have been: supercharged
with transcendent reality and meaning. Think of the gospel
writers' work analogously to the work of Renaissance painters:
the Virgin Mary swathed in brocade, sitting in a drawing room
to receive the great-winged angel Gabriel. The real, literal, historical Mary wore homespun clothes and lived in a hut, and God
has no need of great-winged creatures to carry messages. But
both the painters and the evangelists were trying to capture what
was *really* happening.

Yet the gospel accounts are not mere fabrications. Scholars
discern a quite trustworthy historical framework beneath any
later incrustations or interpretations. Clustered within each of
the gospels are parables Jesus obviously *made up* to clarify his
teaching, as well as stories which most nonscholars might uncritically accept as fact but which probably never literally occurred.
Just as Jesus did with his parables, later minds made up stories to
do the same thing: clarify the truth *beneath* the story. Whether
the wise men actually arrived with their fabulous gifts at Jesus'
birth is hardly the point; the truth the story embodies is that
Jesus came not only for poor, illiterate, Jewish shepherds but also
for wealthy, learned Gentile foreigners.

The evangelists were probably not eyewitnesses. They
gathered and edited previously existing materials and oral sources
around the time the actual eyewitnesses were beginning to die
out. Any historian does the same thing, garnering whatever
scraps of memories they can, validating stories with more than
one witness, fitting the pieces together. When more and more
information began to be available, Matthew and Luke brought
out new editions of Mark.

We can accept with high probability that, indeed, a carpenter
named Jesus, just as a camel driver named Mohammed, actually
existed and believed themselves summoned by God on a holy
mission. We can accept that, like Mohammed, Jesus was tempted

to believe his mission was self-delusive, but that nonetheless he set forth, trusting it. When he was rejected by the people of his own town, he made his headquarters in Capernaum, where he gathered disciples and taught them and the local people a message of freedom from the captivity of material goods, the value of compassion, nonviolence, antilegalism. His ability to cure illnesses and charismatic confidence made him a threat to the establishment, despite his repeated repudiations of worldly ambitions. On his final journey to Jerusalem, he was initially hailed as the Son of David (a requirement for the long-awaited Messiah), and before the Passover Sabbath he celebrated a final meal with his friends at which he gave them bread and said, "This is my body," and a cup of wine and said, "This is my blood." Later, in a garden, agents of the Temple arrested him and took him to their superiors. At the trial, the high priest asked forthrightly, "Are you the Christ, the Son of the Blessed?" And with equal forthrightness, Jesus replied, "I am." Instantly, the high priest tore his garments in shock at such a blasphemy. He was condemned on the spot and sent off to the Roman governor, the only one with powers to execute. After some waffling, Pontius Pilate condemned him, not on a charge of blasphemy but of sedition. Jesus was executed by crucifixion, died, and was buried in a cave. But his followers claimed that a few days later they had experienced Jesus alive again. It is also objective fact that many of them went to horrible deaths rather than deny that experience of the risen Jesus or to stop preaching his message.

We can rely, then, on scholars to show us the different layers of the gospels—historically credible events, plus stories Jesus himself fabricated to prove a point, plus miracles and stories that may or may not have been fabricated later for the same purpose. Thus, we can trust the gospels to mediate reliable truth *if* we can rely on the truth of the resurrection. It all comes down to the resurrection.

The Divinity of Jesus

Jesus did not leave us the option to dismiss him, as many would prefer, as a very fine human being and moral teacher, but hardly anything more. You don't crucify someone whose only message is that we love one another. That's precisely the kind of sheep bureaucrats *want*. This Jesus defied the officials of his religion; he even second-guessed the great Moses! He violated the Sabbath with what he claimed was a higher authority. But the greatest evidence of the grandiosity of his claims about himself came at that trial before the Jewish elders. When the high priest asked, "Are you the Christ? The Son of the Blessed?" he was asking Jesus if he was in fact the promised Messiah and, further than that, the Son of God. And Jesus answered, "I *am*"—words no orthodox Jew would use, because "I am" is the name of God. Even today good Jews will not even write the word in any other form but "G-d." So, of course, in fury at the blasphemy, the high priest tore his garments and saw there was no more need of witnesses. The man had condemned himself out of his own mouth.

The previous Sunday, the crowds had cheered this man through the streets, hailing him as the new Messiah. The following Friday the *same* crowds were screaming, "Crucify him! Crucify him!" There is the reason. He had claimed not only to be *a* son of God but *the* Son of God.

There are only three responses to this: Either Jesus was a madman who thought he was the embodiment of God, as some think they are reincarnations of Napoleon, or he was a conniving fake trying to work the crowds, or he was who he claimed to be. Yet nothing he said or did suggests someone deranged. In fact, when Gandhi was asked what he thought of Christianity, he said, "I think it's absolutely wonderful. I just wish someone would *try* it." Nor does there seem to be anything about this man which was manipulative. He never worked a miracle to provoke faith in him but only in *response* to it. He profited not at all: he had no home or income and only the clothes on his back. The only other alternative is that he was who he claimed to be.

Thus, we can rely on Jesus' claim to divinity *if* we can rely on the resurrection.

The Resurrection

The gospels record no witnesses at the actual resurrection, the moment when the stone rolled back and Jesus came forth alive again. It would have been a simple matter to "stage" a real audience-grabber: thunder, rocks cracking, and Jesus steps forward in a blaze of light! But they didn't. We have only the word of the many people who claim to have experienced Jesus alive again. How can they be trusted? The only substantial answer to this question is the one given before: They went to their deaths, when denial of their claim would have set them free.

At the time of Jesus' execution, the gospels declare—very honestly and self-damningly—his disciples panicked. They fled to the room of the Last Supper and locked themselves in. They were, in a word, flagrant cowards. At that shattering moment of Jesus' defeat, the Church had—to all intents and purposes—ceased to exist. Yet fifty days later, on Pentecost, they emerged ablaze with courage! A courage unto death. It's hard, at least for me, to witness so many people manifest such courage, for so long, and even into death—for a *hoax?* Like their Master, they made no profit from their preaching, only persecution and death.

Something earth-shattering must have occurred to account for such a radical conversion from craven cowards to unflinching apostles. They claim that experience was encountering the risen Jesus. And for most of them, their testimony was a "death-bed confession." I, at least, have to accept their word.

Add to all this the growth of the Christian community since that time, from a handful of fishermen and peasants to a worldwide body of believers. It is miraculous that any merely human organization could last so long, withstanding not only attacks from without but also outlasting its own enormous errors corroding it from within: the early battles over the true nature of Jesus, schisms, the Inquisition, the Crusades—to name only a few of many. The magnitude of the spiritual change this Mustard Seed effected, the profound way in which it changed history, so suddenly and yet so permanently, simply can't be explained by the ardor of a few disciples.

Jesus' Personality

Mothers tell children not to judge people by their looks. Many of us tried, but we find that at times we just can't help it. The image, the firsthand impression, makes it very difficult for unattractive people to find acceptance, not only for who they truly are but for what they say. In that regard, I can think of no greater disservice to the Christian enterprise than the work of second-rate artists and even first-rate filmmakers. Earlier films like DeMille's and even *Jesus of Nazareth* almost without exception pictured him as white, blue-eyed, pale, delicate, and most definitely otherworldly. Such pictures do not show that Jesus was clearly male, much less human. Later films, like *The Last Temptation of Christ, Jesus Christ: Superstar,* and *Godspell,* make him almost solely human, such a simpering wimp he can't even make up his mind about anything at all. (In *Superstar,* Jesus doesn't make a curtain call.) If this is your image of him, you quite likely won't spend much time getting to know him or listening to what he says. Would anyone (especially any male) want to invite such a personage home for brunch after Mass?

Of course, all such religious art is a lie. Well-intentioned, perhaps (to make us good, gentle boys and girls), but still a lie. Jesus couldn't have looked like that. He was a Jew; swarthy skin, dark eyes, out in blistering sun all day. Look at a carpenter's body sometime, especially his hands. Jesus was flogged with leaded whips, battered around, booted through the streets, stretched out with his raw back in the gravel and spiked to the beam of a cross. And he lasted three hours! Hard to see the holy-card Jesus enduring all that.

Such untrue religious art emphasizes only the "feminine" side of Jesus, which was truly there, as it should be in all well-rounded males: kindness, gentleness, sensitivity, approachability—especially to the needy and to children. But there is another whole side to Jesus which is in the gospels but which doesn't get into much church art or biblical movies (or hymns)—his "masculine" side: aggressiveness, authority, decisiveness, confidence.

To give credit to those who hanged Christ, they didn't execute him because he was so gentle. He claimed to be God, and he refused to be quiet about it. He declined to show deference to men of pedigree and position. "The Sabbath was made for people, not people for the Sabbath." He called his priests rather uncomplimentary names: "snakes, whitewashed tombs, blind guides fit for hell"—among others. He had a profound dislike for hypocrisy, especially among the well-placed, and never missed a chance to point it out. He faced down madmen and demons. He worked miracles with any means that came to hand, including mud and spit, and with shocking disregard for other people's swine. He rousted the money changers from the Temple with only a handful of rope and his own moral indignation. He most definitely did not always turn the other cheek himself, not when there was need for rage. At the end, he—like us—was tempted to despair, yet he clung on with faith, and hope, and sheer guts. If this man is boring, I don't know who on God's earth could be called interesting.

But well-meaning churchfolk have "softened" him into

acceptability, made him unthreatening, as Dorothy Sayers writes, "a fit pet for pale curates and pious old ladies." The Lamb of God has devoured the Lion of Judah.

Christian Moral Doctrine

Many elements of Jesus' teaching are common staples of Jewish thought, such as the Great Commandment: "Love God and love your neighbor." But they assume a quite different force powered by the voice that uttered them: "No man has preached like this man." What's more, he changed the elements of this statement profoundly.

In Jesus' teaching, God is totally unlike the Eastern image of God; God is not only "Father," but *Abba:* "Daddy." He is to be held in awe, but trusted. Jesus embodied the nature of God, definitively, in the father of the prodigal son. When the boy requests his inheritance, the father gives it to him, no strings— as God gives us existence and freedom. When the boy has wasted his patrimony and come to his senses, he starts home, memo- rizing an apology. But the father sees the boy from afar off—because the father has been looking for him every day. And the father runs to the boy, not the other way round. He throws his arms around the boy and kisses him *before* the boy can get out his apology! *All* the son had to do was head for home. The father doesn't ask for a catalogue of sins by species and number; his son who was dead is alive again! That's all that matters to this father. And he doesn't give the boy a retaliatory penance. He gives him a party! That is the God of Jesus—though, tragically, often distorted by his interpreters.

In Jesus' teaching, the meaning of neighbor is far different from the rabbinic restrictions on the use of the word. For them, "neighbor" could legitimately be limited, of course, to Jews. Further, it could exclude those who were unclean—lepers, prostitutes, tax collectors, as well as those whose religious practice was shoddy, different from the Temple's format, or nonexistent. Jesus upended that, too. When a lawyer asked what was needed to achieve eternal life, fulfillment, righteousness, the lawyer already knew the answer: Love God, love my neighbor. But the lawyer wanted to know who his neighbor was. If Jesus answered clearly: everyone, especially the outcasts, the lawyer would have turned on his heel. But Jesus trapped him with a story: the Good Samaritan. It wasn't the priest or the Levite who loved the neighbor, but an outcast, someone any decent Jew would say deserved to be kicked into a ditch himself.

If all Christian scriptures and all commentaries and references to love of neighbor were annihilated, and we had just those two stories—the Prodigal Son and the Good Samaritan, I believe we could clone out the entire moral doctrine of Jesus: forgiveness and compassion. The whole gospel story is a record of Jesus' relentless drive not to accuse but to forgive, and the sole question at the Judgment to determine our lives' worth will be only about our compassion.

This is why the term "Christian morality" makes no sense to me. Christianity *presumes* justice. There is no justice in the stories of the Prodigal Son or the Good Samaritan. Until one understands this, one has no idea whatever what Christianity even means.

The Non-Negotiables

Sincere Christians differ about the Real Presence in the Eucharist, the authority of the papacy, the place of the Virgin Mary. They disagree about not-trivial-but-less-definitive issues like birth control, celibate clergy, the role of women. Still, I believe that, beneath the doctrinal abrasions, there are some nonnegotiables of Christian doctrine. You may deny them (as

Gandhi and Camus did) and still be an incandescently good human being, perhaps even a saint. But you can't legitimately call yourself Christian. At the risk of hubris, I offer only four.

(1) Jesus is the embodiment of the Son of God. Somehow—who knows or cares how?—God focused himself out of the time-free and space-free Fifth Dimension into a Nazareth carpenter, to show us how God wants us to live our lives.

(2) Jesus / God died in *order* to rise and to (a) share with us a realization of our own immortality and (b) offer us a share in the divine aliveness (grace).

(3) To incorporate ourselves into Jesus/God we have to find the values of the Kingdom (them first) more important than the values of the World (me first).

(4) We embody this union in (a) a serving community and (b) a weekly meal of gratitude.

There, I think, you have at least the core: the Incarnation, the Resurrection, Antimaterialism, Service, and Eucharist. For twenty centuries, theologians have bickered and battled (and even brained!) one another over how to fine-tune even those bare four beliefs. How could Jesus be both human and divine? How could God be Father and Son and Spirit? What does grace really mean and how do we avail ourselves of it? What really takes place in the Eucharist? All these are very high-powered and perhaps important questions for some who enjoy such rarefied pursuits. But I don't think the majority of ordinary Christians need to trouble themselves with them—or with any of thousands of other even more arcane conundrums. If those good people can sort of grasp and buy into and find their lives enriched by just those four basic beliefs, I think that's just *fine*. And I have a perhaps-presumptuous hunch that Jesus would be pleased, too.

As we have seen more than once, the essence of Christianity is distilled in a crucifix: a man utterly used up for others, drained even of his last drop of blood. The genuine Christian looks at this and says, "There is the most perfectly fulfilled human being who ever lived, caught at the moment of his greatest triumph. I want to be like him."

If this gospel doesn't unnerve you, you've never really heard it before.

Questions to Ponder and Discuss

⚹ Most of us are more at ease with formulas, mathematical or logical, rather than symbols and stories, to explain the nearly unexplainable, whether it is the inner workings of the atom or the causes of inflation. We are not at all as comfortable with stories like *The Color Purple* or *A Catcher in the Rye* or *The Sparrow* answering the question "What are people for?" Do you have personal hesitations about accepting the stories in the gospels as mediating truth rather than *explicitating* historical truth? How much would it trouble your faith, say, to admit that Peter never literally walked on water but that the core of the story is true: If you keep your eyes on Jesus and forget your shortcomings, you can do what you thought was impossible, perhaps not walk on water but be crucified upside down rather than deny your experience of Jesus risen?

⚹ Reread the argument trying to establish a basis for trusting Jesus' divinity. Does it ring true, or do you have hesitations about it? Try to poke holes in it. This is what genuine learning is for. Think up arguments against it to challenge your instructors. Their task is to make you reach for better answers than you had previously settled for. Now's the time to return the favor.

✦ The fact of Jesus' resurrection is absolutely crucial. If it is a pipe dream, everything to do with Christianity (except its laudable inducements to forgiveness and compassion) are "straw." Can you in your innermost self submit to the probability that the disciples were telling the truth? Can you admit—with no *reasonable* doubt—that Jesus actually did, in *some* way, manifest himself to his disciples after he had been certifiably dead? If not, the only other alternative is that the atheist argument is right: When you have a flat EKG, that's all there is.

✦ The text has made a strong point that our understanding of Jesus' doctrine is undercut by our physical image of Jesus and our apprehension of the kind of personality he was. Has your long-standing picture of Jesus been as overly "feminized" and under "masculinized" as the text suggests? If so, what readjustments need to be made in your mind about the person we all suspect may be the embodiment of what God wanted human beings to become all along?

✦ The text has also been consistently making a point of the meaninglessness of "Christian morality." Does this make any sense? Have you always thought "Christianity" and "morality" mean the same thing? Explain, at least to yourself, why they are not.

✦ Try to find somewhere in the skeletalized outline of the non-negotiables of Christianity where you would find something *essential* missing, something that any Christian of whatever denomination would find lacking, something that Jesus would feel has been left out. (If you find something, write me about it. I still have a lot to learn about Christianity, too.)

✦ Scripture: Deuteronomy 7:8-10; Luke 10:26-28; Romans 3:8-10; 8:3; Galatians 3:23-29; 5:14; 6:1-3

✦ *Catechism:* 864, 1823-1825, 2069, 2196

All the boats leak. The only question is:
Which boat leaks least?

—Walter Kuhn

✤ 8 ✤

WHY BE CATHOLIC?

A high school senior once asked me, "Do you think there are a lot of [serious flaws] in the Catholic Church?" I answered without a flicker, "Of course! And I know more 'serious flaws' than you do." "Then," he asked, with a bit more acid than I liked, "why don't you leave? You're a hypocrite." I confess his acid infected my reply: "That's moronic." And he snapped back, "You calling me a moron?" I almost said, "Why not? You just called me a hypocrite." Instead, I said, "I didn't call *you* a moron; I called that *idea* moronic. I also see a lot of flaws in the way our government embodies the ideal of American democracy. But not enough to make me pack up and emigrate to Fiji."

If anyone has serious problems accepting the Roman Catholic Church, I'd suggest—for their own sake—they sit down and list them on a piece of paper, rather than letting them ramble around their minds, unfocused, vague and embittering. Really dredge them up. Then go back and cross out all the truly trivial ones: "A priest once bawled me out"; "I know some hypocritical churchgoers"; "How was Mary bodily lifted outside time and space into a way of being that's not a place and where bodies don't exist?" One consistent objection is, "All those rules!" But when pressed, the objector is usually hard-pressed to specify what those rules are. Other than the ones that seem to overemphasize sexuality, what other specific rules do you find insupportable? Finally, sort through the cut-down list and ask how many remaining objections result from idealistic expectations no *humanly* embodied institution could satisfy.

The premise of this chapter is that there is no perfect church—not when it's an ideal embodied by human beings who are, by definition, imperfect. As Walter Kuhn says, "All the boats leak. The only question is, which boat leaks least?" In what follows we'll explore why I think the Catholic Church is the least leaky boat. But first, why do we need communal religion at all? Kids ask that, right? Why? If the liturgy is unengaging, the problem is not always with the "script" or with the "performers." The word "religion" means "a binding fast," a person-to-person connection between the worshiper and God, and the word "Eucharist" means "thanksgiving." If the person in the pew experiences no connection to God except in that one hour a week and takes the gift of existence (and all that it entails) for granted, there is no way the liturgy can be spiritually energizing.

Substitute Religions

The volatile brew generated by the events of the sixties left us older Catholics infected with skepticism. Assassinations, Vietnam, Watergate, hostages, terrorism (to name only a few) made anyone who put trust in anything beyond family and a few friends look naive. Surely one would be a fool to put faith in any earthly institution. All riddled with self-serving, close-minded bureaucrats, each with his or her blind need to dominate, who treat the rest of us like gullible sheep.

The Church fared no better. Priests, nuns, even bishops left their ministries; the official Church seemed at odds with many respected theologians. Today, surveys indicate that 80 percent of churchgoing Catholics practice artificial birth control despite the inescapable fact that the official Church clearly believes it immoral; bishops differ publicly with one another over condoms as a lesser evil than AIDS. The list is nearly endless. As even the most inexperienced investor knows, "When the management's at odds with itself, invest somewhere else, or not at all."

Yet a lot of the people who drifted away from organized religion then are now drifting back. Why? Because the belief systems the disaffected chose to substitute for religion simply didn't do the job. Casual sex, psychotherapy, getting to the top, primal scream, crusading for causes—they just didn't work as religious substitutes. That's because none of them, not even all of them together, have it within themselves to deliver for very long our basic need: the enduring conviction of personal worth. Who am I? Where do I fit into all this?

A God-Sized Hunger

Religion substitutes are like junk food for the body and sitcoms for the soul; they assuage our hunger for meaningful lives—for a moment—but they give no sense of coherence, of being "at home" in our own skins and in the relationships around us. Underneath our busyness and distractions, those dark questions are still nagging at the core of our souls: "Why? Why do people suffer? Why would a good God give freedom to a tribe of apes inadequately evolved to use it wisely? Why must we die? Is that all there is?" One boy put it very tersely: "Without God, life's an Easter egg hunt. And there are no Easter eggs." There is still a hunger unsatisfied: the desire to plug into the Power that energizes it all. Saint Augustine probably said it best: "Our hearts are restless till they rest in You."

Beyond that, too, is a realization of how blessed we have been, with all the things we so easily take for granted—existence itself, for example. If God opened the door to, well . . . everything, then how indebted we are! Sometime (especially when you're feeling sorry for yourself and least want to do it) sit down and picture in your mind the people you love most. Dwell on each face for as long as the pleasure lasts, then pass on to the next, and the next. Move beyond that most intimate circle to people who give you laughs, make you think, pat you on the back. Without that initial gift of existence, you never would have known any of them. Granted, if you'd never been born, you'd never know the difference. But you *were* born, and how precious they all are! How impoverished you'd be without them! It would seem any honorable person would be eager to say thanks for that first, sine-qua-non gift. The word "Eucharist" *means* thanksgiving, gratitude.

Many who genuinely acknowledge an inner need for the ultimate connection argue that one ought to be able just to go out into the woods or onto a mountain peak and commune with the enlivening presence of God. My first response to that is, "Fine! When was the last time you actually *did* it?" But another, less bristly response is: "Why either/or? Why not both?" In fact, worshiping God together is far more enlivened for those for whom it is not their only contact with God in seven days. It's as ludicrous to walk into a church "cold" and anticipate getting zapped as it is to expect the same dazzling effect on a first date.

The genuine hermits among us are few. We need one another. The worst punishment a human can endure—perhaps more painful than liberating death—is solitary confinement.

What's more, having others worshiping with you (however apparently insulated) does give a feeling that you're not the only one. Even further, we have a need to *feel* (not just know) that we're not alone, that we have a communally held notion of what it's all about, what we're groping toward, what explosive effect on our solitary lives comes from our adoption, together, into the Trinity Family.

If Jesus embodies the will of God for us, then we have no right to stay huddled in the Upper Room, much less in our private isolated cocoons. Just like his first disciples, we are *sent*, as a serving community, out into the highways and byways to find the indifferent, the dulled, the bored and to invite them into that community which celebrates each week that we no longer dread death, no longer anguish over our guilt, no longer fear the world is all on our shoulders alone. And we offer a Food whose sole purpose is to assuage that God-sized hunger.

"All right. I'll admit I need other people. But why be Catholic? Why not Lutheran or Methodist or Anglican?" No problem with that at all. If you're really serious about it (unlike those people who propose praying in the woods but never do), there are encyclopedias aplenty. Just haul down a few volumes and read about each one. Test them out, like Goldilocks, to see which are too hard, which too soft, and which "just right." Then maybe even attend a service or two, meet some churchgoers and talk to them.

Fair warning, however: Don't expect the *realities* of any of the churches to live up to the idealistic descriptions. Any student knows his or her real school is quite unlike the glowing description in the brochure. Ideals, like the North Star, are guides, not destinations. Any ideal—even the Gospel—is going to have an embarrassing mess of loopholes and shoddy spots and "not-quites" and downright scandals when embodied by human beings, with their own axes to grind, vested interests, and blind spots. If you want an ideal church, best try another planet.

There are many embodiments of the Christian belief, but it seems inescapable that—no matter what its faults—the Roman Catholic Church does seem to be the "original." No one would or could say Rome broke away from the Orthodox or Lutherans or Calvinists or Anglicans. Perhaps their allegations were right, that the "original" had become so corrupt and irremediable that they had to secede and start over. Nonetheless, again and again, because the Spirit of God is still alive in her, the Church has humbled herself before the error of her ways and come back home—exactly like the Israel God refused to give up on.

One of the oldest metaphors for the Church is Peter's fishing boat. Good insights into the Church are packed into that metaphor: We're on a journey—together—with a map, lots of stormy weather, people slipping overboard, survivors being pulled in, mutinies among the crew, getting off course, being attacked by pirates. And a boat needs a captain when everybody's losing their heads. He may not be the ideal captain—too lax, too strict, too single-minded (like Ahab in *Moby Dick*), but if everybody grabs for the tiller we're all in trouble. Then again, for quite some time Peter wasn't ideal either, yet what his crew managed to make has lasted two thousand years.

Jesus intended the Church he founded, quite clearly, to reach out as far as possible, "to the ends of the earth," and to embrace women and men of all shades of political attitude, race, language, social position, color. To unite this transcultural entity, as with any society, there has to be a single director, perhaps less inflexible about uniformity than many popes have been, but more than a mere figurehead symbol like the Queen of England.

Orthodox, Protestant, and Anglican traditions all are surely holy and trace their history ultimately back to the root Christian Church. But Orthodox seem (at least to me) too nationally and geographically divided, and—to be honest—their liturgies are at least twice too long. Knowing what I know from Jesus in the gospels, I don't feel at all "at home" with the Protestant belief in total human depravity, even after the sacrifice of Jesus. As far as I can discern, their God is not as unconditionally forgiving as the God of Jesus seems to be. Moreover, with almost uncountable separate groups, Protestantism seems not a church but many churches. Except for a few, their ritual doesn't even claim to transform: only to "remind." Anglicans have a lot of compassion and flexibility, and yet their flexibility seems (to me) too diverse, and I always come up short on the fact that, no matter what their doctrinal quibbles, the true reason for their separation from Rome was the fact that the autocratic Henry VIII wanted a son and couldn't get a divorce. Again, this is primarily personal, a matter only partly of the rational left brain and far more rooted in the intuitive right brain: "This one is too hard. This one is too soft. This one is . . . well, not perfect but more comfortable than any other I've tried so far."

No matter what my differences from the opinions of various popes, the papacy is a force in my life. In the hurly-burly of materialism, exploitation, capitalistic and socialistic saber rattling, there is always a focal, powerful figure who comes forward to remind us what we are: human beings ennobled by Christ. The pope is, for me, a father. I don't always agree with my father. But I need one. At the Mass Pope John Paul II celebrated in Central Park, one feminist, liberal, nonpracticing reporter looked at him, shrugged, and said, "Who else have we got?"

Many of us need a pope for "trustworthy guidelines," words which lack the consoling and inflexible certitude of "dogma." I'm not at all comfortable with dogma, since—other than "We will all die"—I can think of almost no statement that couldn't admit of at least *some* exceptions. Nonetheless, I'm content with solid-but-admittedly-still-imperfect. Such answers are not just not bad; they're the best we're going to get. My faith is not seriously disturbed (though some few, most of them quite

powerful, would strongly disagree) to admit that "the Church"—
or at least those who speak definitively in her name—has been
wrong. Saint Paul was wrong about slavery and women;
Augustine was wrong about sex; the popes were wrong about the
crusades, the Inquisition, Galileo, not to mention at least some
of the more recent internal controversies. Why not admit the
inescapable truth rather than try to project an image of "the
flawless parent"? Once we admit the mistakes, then we can
forgive them, as we would do in any family, as Jesus surely would
do. But until one admits a mistake, one doesn't head for home
and forgiveness.

We need a pope, but the pope also needs the people, and not
just for spiritual and financial support, but for ideas—and for a
forthright critique of his ideas. There are two kinds of authority.
Political authority is conferred by election or inheritance or sheer
brute force: the pope and bishops, the chairman of the board, the
cop on the beat. *Moral* authority is not conferred but achieved,
by study or experience or sheer bloody endurance: the theologian, the long-time teacher, people who have been married for
years. They are different but *complementary* and genuine kinds of
authority. The man or woman in the pew may not have a
doctorate in theology, but then again the pope has never been
married. In order for the Body of Christ to survive—much less
avoid an endless un-civil war within itself—it needs the diverse
wisdom of all of its parts.

And what about the prodigals? I doubt anyone can "leave the
Church," any more than one can "leave" his or her family. When
the prodigal son left home to seek his own way without his
father's interference, he may have left the house, but he didn't
stop being a member of that family. He may have been a remiss
and ungrateful son; he may never have written or come for a visit
on the holidays. But he never stopped being a son of that father
or a part of that unique family. He could no more forswear his

family than he could reject his DNA. As they said of James Joyce, "You can take the boy out of the Church, but you can't take the Church out of the boy." They may be "nonpracticing Catholics," but they're still Catholics.

A major practical problem, however, arises for such people (as any priest knows too well) at those key moments in human life that are just too "big" for anyplace else but a church. Birth, marriage, and death—these are moments when God is no longer escapable, when this event has to be *celebrated!* At these times it's not sufficient merely to go to a Justice of the Peace's office or issue a birth or death certificate. We have to put the event into some far greater context. That's when the prodigals head for home.

But I, at least, have some difficulty with those "flying visits home," like the prodigal son returning *not* to apologize but to have his mother do the laundry, put the arm on his father for a bit of cash, and wing right out again not to be heard from again till he is in need. For many who ask for baptism, marriage or Christian burial with Mass, there is every indication this is a one-time thing. I find it difficult as a priest to induct children into a "club" in which their own parents take no significant interest. I find it difficult to offer a wedding Mass which is of itself only an excuse for dressing up and flowers and a thundering organ—less important to the couple than the photographs. If a man or woman dies having led their lives in reasonable peace about their lack of overt religion, I find it a violation of the deceased's conscience (and my own) to offer them Christian burial merely to ease their relatives' consciences.

At those times, I ask those requesting Mass to sit down and write out for me why they want a priest there—not me as an old friend, but any priest. It often has most salutary results. Most nonpracticing Catholics are not mean-spirited. They're just too busy with what seem like far more important matters than their God-sized hunger.

Conversely, consistent religious practice doesn't decidedly embody genuine religion. The kids love this one: "I know this guy who goes to Mass every week, and he's a true SOB." Right. But how much worse an SOB might he be if he *didn't* worship every week? More important, I have a tough enough time evaluating my own motives; how do I evaluate someone else's? But these porcupine kids have a point. We all know people who are consistent churchgoers who are nonetheless judgmental, arrogant, mean-spirited—perhaps even clerics, who are professional Christians. They've got us there.

Religion means "to bind fast," a person-to-Person "connection," whether the liturgical performance is lackluster or jubilant, whether the priest is overacting or dull. If your connection isn't real, the text could be written by Toni Morrison, the hymns by Leonard Bernstein, delivered by a priest with the combined gifts of Walter Cronkite and Robin Williams, but there is no real religion. Can I *see* your freedom? Can I *feel* your joy? Perhaps the obstacle is you.

If you give it an honest chance, the Mass—not just the externals but what we allow to transpire within our souls—can be a reminder that our innermost selves live not merely in our day-to-day involvements but also beyond time and space, right now! If we can just let go the pretenses and defenses, the messed-up priorities, we can begin to understand our true selves, members of the Body of Christ, animated by the divine Spirit.

A Bipolar Church

Doubtless Catholic intellectuals slapped around the labels "liberal" and "conservative" in earlier days, but the ordinary practitioner wasn't aware of them. Now they're commonplace. The solid, impregnable, unified Church which was so appealing then seems at odds with itself now.

But those who concentrate relentlessly on our differences in liturgical style, in doctrinal and disciplinary disputes, in attitudes toward the official Church, miss something very important. In fact, a miracle! We're all still *here!* Even though we go on batting one another like fractious children, none of us wants to leave the Trinity Family. There's something more important than our peculiar "stances" on questions. Being Catholic!

Despite the fact that attendance dropped from 70 percent to 40 percent, that 40 percent remnant is going to Mass *without* the sanction of mortal sin: 15 to 20 million Catholics, middle-class, educated, actively participating not only in worship but in volunteer activities, committed, informed, energetic. Active Catholics are still the largest single religious body in the United States. Our antagonisms would fade to mere irritations, I think, if we just stood back and looked at what the Church *should* be.

I once wrote a book about the Church I wanted to call *The Big, Bad, Beautiful Balancing Rock* (which the publisher wisely changed to *Why Be Catholic?*). I copped the idea from Chesterton, who said the true Church is not some immovable bulwark but a huge ugly rock with all manner of knobs and excrescences, pivoting precariously on its pedestal. The excesses of the conservative delicately balance the overindulgences of the liberal. Not only is difference of opinion unavoidable, it's *essential!* Let the quietist seek a liturgy without hymns and the enthusiast find one that rocks. Let us content ourselves with a church that is "home" both to William F. Buckley and Anna Quindlan.

It is, I believe, pharisaic to scoff at "cafeteria Catholics," who choose which doctrines they find themselves able to accommodate with the rest of what they know. In the course of history, under the guidance of the Holy Spirit, the magisterium of the Church evolved as a guide in doctrinal and disciplinary matters. But we must not forget that God also gave each of us intelligence, and one presumes God intended us to use it. We can still achieve balance as a Church if we all accept what seem the non-negotiables on which our Rock pivots: that Jesus is the Son of God, who died and rose in order to assure us of our immortality and to share divine aliveness (grace) with us, that the values of the Kingdom far outweigh the values of the world, that we celebrate our incorporation into Christ in a serving community and in a weekly meal at which Christ is more truly present than anywhere else on earth. This is what unites us. Theologians and church officials may differ on the finer points of doctrine. Individuals may differ in their sense of which Church teachings are unquestionable, in their response to the hierarchy or to styles of worship. But, despite our differences, we are still the one People of God. When I grew up, I disagreed strongly with my dad about Jews, but that didn't make us love one another less.

The Educated Catholic

The malaise of many cradle Catholics about changes in the liturgy (which sounds like "metallurgy"), the dress and demeanor of priests and nuns, the loss of solid certitudes, arose at least partly from substituting faith in the institutional Church for faith itself, for the message of the Gospel, and even for a genuine person-to-Person connection with God. The problem was never Latin or lack of participation, but faith itself, inability to articulate our belief to ourselves, not in others' formulas but in our own words.

The official Church is, undeniably, a powerful voice in the formation of any Catholic's beliefs. But there are other sources which can also enrich those same beliefs: our new understanding of cosmology, psychology, anthropology, not to mention the complementary insights from other world religions into the vital connection between humans and the Ultimate (which is what "religion" means). This relationship cannot be definitively encapsulated in formulas and disciplines. It also requires a tolerance for ambiguity, since mystery is the very essence of our individual and communal dealings with God.

Close to the core of our God-sized hunger is what Eugene Kennedy calls "mystery deprivation." In a true sense, "all those changes" have left religion disenchanted—stripped not only of superstitious illusions but also of exhilarating potency. We are dealing with realities beyond intellectual discernment but directly accessible to intuition. We don't need to "define" it, to "master the data," any more than we can encompass love or humor. We can only experience it. Therefore, perhaps the first best step for anyone doubtful of Catholicism is a weekend retreat.

We serve a God who, demonstrably, is restless with stasis. Surely the upward process of evolution shows that. In each of us natural crises call us from security to larger lives: birth, weaning, play years, school, adolescence, dating, marriage, old age, death. The Bible proves it as well: God shows up just as his people settle into security, whistling them out onto the road again. Jesus stops by the disciples' skiffs, upending their expectations of themselves. The pattern of God's preferences for growth and change seems inescapable.

Of all ecclesiastical boats, it strikes me that the Barque of Peter leaks least, and for all its faults and confusions, no matter how others have rearranged the furniture, banished comforting customs, roller-coastered from majestic to folksy, to pallid, to engaging, it's still "home," still my peevish, cantankerous, thin-skinned family, still that big old, bad old, beautiful old balancing rock.

Questions to Ponder and Discuss

❧ Suppose you had the opportunity for a no-holds-barred (tactful) meeting with the pope. Make a list, in no particular order at first, of the matters you'd like to take up with him. Take all the time you want. But when you finish, a papal official reminds you that you will have exactly fifteen minutes with the Holy Father, no more but no less. Now narrow your list to the absolutely most important questions. Then bring them to your instructional team.

❧ Saint Paul writes, "The eye cannot say to the hand, 'I don't need you!' Nor can the head say to the feet, 'Well, I don't need you!' On the contrary, we cannot do without the parts of the body that seem to be weaker; and those parts that we think aren't worth very much are the ones we treat with greater care" (I Corinthians 12:21-22). How does that insight into the Church, the Body of Christ, apply to our differences of opinion in liturgical style, in doctrinal and disciplinary disputes, in attitudes toward the official Church? Can the conservative say to the liberal, "I don't need you!"—or vice versa? Can ordinary Catholics say to their bishop, "Well, I don't need you!"—or vice versa? Can any of us say to the panhandler on the street, "Well, I don't need you"?

❧ "All the boats leak. The only question is, which boat leaks least?" Very honestly, can you be content with a church which is not as perfect as many want it to be? This question was purposely misworded, simply because—this side of heaven—a perfect church is impossible. The point of the question is: Can you *resign* yourself to a church whose people (high and low) are more often than we'd like peevish, nit-picking, overbearing, self-righteous, pushy, single-minded, fainthearted—*if* we all genuinely do hold the nonnegotiables, together? Is it possible to put our fussy disputes over less important issues and questions into perspective when we agree on the essentials? Think of a single concrete dispute, say, over liturgical style, sexual practice, attitude to the Vatican. Now, picture two Catholics you know who hold strongly opposing views on this question, and imagine them arguing it out at the foot of the cross where Jesus hangs, dying.

✤ Consider a specific case. A young man comes to a priest who taught him ten years before, asking if the priest will officiate at his wedding. He's marrying a Jewish woman and has agreed to bring up the children as Jews, not for religious reasons but rather ethnic ones. Is he still a practicing Catholic? Well, no. How long since he's been to Mass? Two or three years. Does he still pray? Not really. Well, why does he want a priest to solemnize his wedding? You don't stop being Catholic. And no one can walk through the streets of any big city and not see Christ suffering. But is it really Christ, or is it just your human decency reacting to pain? Well, uh . . . Do *you* really want this Mass to be a Catholic sacrament, or are you asking me just so you can placate your very religious Catholic parents?—If you were the priest, what would you do?

✤ Those of us in our waning years who formed ourselves as Catholics amid the consoling certitudes about the Church during the depression and World War II, then went through the maelstrom ride during and after Vatican II—and are still here— deserve a bit of a hand. It surely shows a faith that can endure storms and uncertainty. But our "days dwindle down to a precious few." Considering the trends moving in the Church today, what unexpected changes will your faith be expected to weather?

✤ Scripture: Matthew 16:13-19; 20:1-16; Ephesians 5:29-30

✤ *Catechism:* 830-856

Maybe the Bible don't read as lively as the scratch sheet, but it is at least twice as accurate.

—Damon Runyon, *Guys and Dolls*

✳ 9 ✴

SCRIPTURE FROM SCRATCH

The late scripture scholar Raymond E. Brown, S.S., wrote:

Because Scripture is inspired and presumably this inspiration was for the good of all, there has arisen the fallacy that everyone should be able to pick up the Bible and read it profitably. If this implies that everyone should be able to find out what the sacred author is saying without preparation or study, it really demands of God in each instance a miraculous dispensation from the limitations imposed by differences of time and circumstance.

—Jerome Biblical Commentary

The primary task of the scriptural authors was to be intelligible *to their own times*. To read the Bible as the authors intended requires that our biblical education be proportionate to our other education. No one would dump *Lear* on beginners without many notes, yet we blithely dump *Luke* on them and expect them to fathom it. Knowing how to read doesn't guarantee one can read either Shakespeare or Scripture with anything more than the vaguest comprehension.

The *Catechism* echoes this same truth: "In order to discover the sacred author's intention, the reader must take into account the conditions of their time and culture, the literary genres in use at that time, and the modes of feeling, speaking, and narrating then current" (109-110).

Before we get to any problems associated with writings of another time and culture, probably the most basic obstacle to understanding Scripture, for both believers and unbelievers, is *literalism:* taking every word and every event as if they were intended by the author to be a straightforward declaration of what actually occurred or an accurate, forthright statement of some truth, clear and plainspoken. Extreme literalists find a great many more problems in the Scriptures than they need to, and surely more than the original writers intended or the original readers confronted. Skeptical literalists (rationalists) take one look at the Tower of Babel, the star of Bethlehem, walking on water, and—reading them as if they actually happened—scoff them away as delusional hogwash. Naive literalists (fundamentalists) blithely accept the talking snake, the mass suicide of the Gadarene swine, multiplication of loaves and fishes, as if they had the same rock-solid verifiability as the assassination of John Kennedy and the Challenger explosion. Thus, they must keep everything religious in the right lobe of the brain, walled off from all they know from paleontology, psychology, and physics in the left lobe.

124 WILLIAM J. O'MALLEY

The author of *Genesis* was no more under the illusion his audience believed snakes once talked to naked ladies in the park than Aesop (writing at about the same time) thought his audience believed tortoises and hares once made bets on impossible races.

Literalists, of either persuasion, miss out on a lot in the Bible. They quite often miss out on jokes, too. Because they have no sense of nuance, irony, symbols, (or humor), they not only are incapable of having fun with language but they miss the meaning *entirely.* "I feel like dirt. My chick gave me my walking papers. She's got a brick for a heart." Incapable of "translating" the figurative language, the literalist replies: "Now, I mean *really.* Dirt has no feelings at all, correct? And you mean to tell me you were dating a *chicken?* And that chicken hopped onto a keyboard and typed out a separation statement? And, my word, if one's heart were made of hardened clay, the person would be dead, wouldn't she? My friend, you're really in need of psychiatric help."

When such people read that Jesus said, "Be perfect as your heavenly Father is perfect," they either try (fundamentalists) to be flawless as God is, and thus end up self-hating masochistic wrecks, or they recognize (rationalists), rightly, the impossibility of flawlessness and walk off with a sneer. Neither realizes that, for a Jew, "perfect" didn't mean without blemish but "whole, all-together," knowing who you are and who God is, and being content. Nor does either of them comprehend that, for a Jew, aspiring to perfection would be blasphemy, since only God can be perfect. They don't realize that's just what the Adam and Eve story is all about!

Hubris didn't mean honest pride; it meant arrogance. "Eternal life" didn't mean just making it into heaven; it meant being right with God *here-and-now.* The Hebrew Scriptures were written in Hebrew; the Christian Scriptures were written in Greek—translated from Aramaic. Do any readers of this book have a Thesaurus to explain the shadings of Hebrew and Greek word-choices? That's why any beginner needs a Bible commentary, to find out what the authors meant to *their* audiences.

Literal language means exactly what it says, e.g., "The roses are blooming in the garden." Figurative language means something different from what it actually says, e.g., "The roses are blooming in your cheeks." Symbolic language can often say *more* than can be said with strictly literal language, just as a painting can often reveal more character than a candid photograph.

Again, what we need is left-brain, right-brain complementarity. On the one hand, there is a definite literal statement under the figurative language: "I feel drained. My girlfriend broke up with me. How could she be so hard-hearted?" On the other hand, you have to have the intuitive "give" that goes *beyond* the words taken literally and tells more. You sense the speaker's *feelings* in the first version of the breakup, which doesn't come through in the second, bland statement.

A further problem, however. Interpretation of the figurative statement has to be *governed* by context and by the acceptable meanings of the words given. A passage from Scripture or Shakespeare isn't a Rorschach test: "Look at these inkblots and tell me what they make you think of." One time with a group of juniors, I did a poem by Amy Lowell, called "Wind and Silver."

> *Greatly shining,*
> *The Autumn moon floats in the thin sky,*
> *And the fishponds shake their backs*
> *And flash their dragon scales*
> *As she passes over them.*
>
> Amy Lowell (1874-1925)

Nothing simpler. Just a picture of a pond, and the moon makes the ripples look like dragon scales. Hand up. "I've got a different interpretation." Okay, as long as the data of the poem support it; it's not a Rorschach Test. "It's about a U-2 flight over Red China." Momentary readjustment of mandible. Where's the evidence? "Right there! 'Dragon scales.'" But you took two words and spun out your own poem! "That's *your* opinion." I tried sarcasm: Why couldn't it be a U-2 flight over medieval England; they had dragons. "That's your opinion." Then I had him: Look at the end of the poem, Amy Lowell, 1874-1925. She was *dead!* There *was* no Red China! There *were* no U-2s! And he said: "That's *your* opinion."

Marya Mannes once said it's too bad learning requires humility but takes place at a time in life when you're most arrogant.

Scripture from Both Sides

Until I was in my thirties, I was completely untroubled accepting everything in the Scripture as literally true. Despite what I knew about cosmology, I had no difficulty accepting that at the ascension Jesus went "up" to heaven, even if the other brain lobe knew that, in the Einsteinian universe, "up" has meaning only relative to where the observer happens to be at the moment, thus an old lady in Australia would go "up" to heaven in exactly the opposite direction.

My first scripture course fissioned all my naive convictions about the Bible. "Father, I know we're not trying to prove the gospel writers knew Jesus, but are we trying to prove they at least knew what they were talking about?" No. (Gasp) You mean original sin, the core of our spiritual lives, isn't rooted with two naked people who fell for a fast-talking snake? Jesus didn't walk on water? And, uh, what about the, uh, resurrection? I remember big-bodied Wally Jungers pacing my tiny room like a caged Minotaur, growling, "If I can't find *some*body who can *prove* to me, beyond a *shadow* of a doubt, Jesus rose from the dead, I'm *outta* this damn place!"

For awhile, the only thing that kept me plodding was that the scripture profs still said Mass. After twenty-five years of exclusively rationalist, Gradgrind education, we finally, painfully had to begin coping with symbols and figurative language, with the differences between literal truth and literary truth, between accurate and meaningful. The evangelists wrote not as historians but to *evangelize*, reporting not what eyewitnesses actually saw but what was actually *happening*—just as renaissance painters picture Mary swathed in brocade or saints with golden haloes tacked to their heads. It didn't matter if the Magi ever showed up; the story is still true—Jesus came not only for poor, illiterate Jews but for rich, learned foreigners too. No need to ask how Peter walked on water; the story is still true—focus on Jesus and forget your own shortcomings, and you can do what you thought impossible, like being crucified rather than deny knowing Jesus risen.

We were forcibly ejected from Plato's comfortable cave of shadows, out into the light.

Figurative Language

We use, receive, and "translate" figurative language every day of our lives, as in the case of the chick with the brick for a heart. But most left all that stuff like hyperbole and irony back in school, where it had no more value than keeping English teachers occupied. On the contrary, if a reader has no sense of those figures of speech, he or she will get scriptural messages all tied up in knots. Perhaps a very quick brush-up course might remind us that we need one. Just as we use figurative language routinely, so did Jesus and the gospel writers.

Hyperbole distorts the literal truth by pushing it to *obviously* absurd exaggeration.

> *I'm gonna kill you, Junior!*

> *It's as easy for a rich man to get into heaven as for a camel to get through the eye of a needle.*

Irony distorts the literal truth by saying the opposite of what one really means.

Nice dress. Salvation Army?

Behold! The King of the Jews!

Paradox distorts the literal truth by making it seem like a contradiction.

Sometimes you have to be cruel to be kind.

If you want the first place, take the last place.

Metaphor is a comparison between two basically unlike things, trying to explain the less known element by analogy to the better known element.

You may not know Alfie, but he's a pig.

The Kingdom of God is like a mustard seed.

Allusion is a comparison to some person or event in literature or history. (Of course, if you have little knowledge of either, especially of mythology and the Hebrew Scriptures, that comparison is not only *not* going to clarify but will usually make you turn the page in frustration.)

Who do you think you are, Ann Landers?

John is the Elijah who was to return.

Taking such statements literally misses the point. If one has no sense of hyperbole, one could get the idea Jesus' statement about the rich man and camel completely forecloses the well-to-do from the Kingdom, since I find it difficult even to poke a tiny thread through the eye of a needle. Well-meaning homilists with prosperous congregations appeal to the "fact" that there was a gate in the Jerusalem wall so narrow that it was called "The Needle's Eye," and a camel could in fact get through if it got rid of its baggage. Nice try. There was no such gate. The parent doesn't mean she's going to *kill* Junior, but she's not just angry at the kid, she's *damn* angry. Just so, the camel hyperbole doesn't mean it's impossible for the wealthy to enter the Kingdom, just *a lot* more difficult than for someone without so many distractions.

We've heard the paradox, "If you want the first place, take the last place" so often it no longer has the power to pull us up short—as "Poetry is a way of saying something that can't be said" might. Again, we think we understand it: "Oh, last place here means first place in heaven." How could someone be both first *and* last in a race—unless he or she were the only contestant? (Close the book a minute and try to figure it out for yourself.) It's quite simple, really: There are two races, each heading 180 degrees in the opposite direction, the Donald Trump race heading toward Beverly Hills and the Jesus race heading to the hill of Calvary. The question isn't where you'll *end up* in the race but which direction you're heading right *now*. Peachy question.

Similarly, a metaphor isn't revealing unless you *decompact* it. "Alfie is a pig." What can you say about pigs (which you do know about) and about Alfie (whom you don't know)? It's not a perfect match-up (no trotters, stove-plate nose, curly tail), but you get a better picture. Just so with the treasure in a field metaphor. Decompact it. (Again, close the book and try it for yourself first.) Okay, you're boppin' along in your field and your toe hits something. You peer down and, lo! It seems to be a box. You paw around it and, whaddya know, it *is* a box. You snap open the lock with a rock, creak open the lid, and WOW! It's filled with diamonds, rubies, coins, pearls. And it's all *yours!* I don't know about you, but I know I'd shout—helplessly—"Holy (BLEEP)!"

Which means that, if you *had* ever actually understood the Good News—that our sins are forgiven and that we need never fear death, you simply *must* have shouted, "Holy (BLEEP)!" And if you haven't, if being Christian hasn't made you feel the same liberating exhilaration a paroled convict feels, then quite likely you haven't even *heard* the Good News yet!

Symbolic Stories

A great many not-yet-convinced Christians are harmed by well-meaning instructors who leave them with the false impression that the Bible is "nothing but a bunch of myths." The teachers haven't realized—or been able to convey—that there are two quite different (in fact contrary) meanings of the word "myth." In the negative sense, "myth" means a false belief uncritically accepted, as in "Vietnam destroyed the myth that America could never lose a war"; objective facts prove that belief a delusion. In the positive sense, "myth" means a story which attempts to express or explain a basic truth, as in Aesop's tale of the turtle and hare: Slow and steady wins the race; and in the story of Adam and Eve and their talking snake: Only human beings go against God's will for them.

Thus, there are two very valid ways of communicating truth: the literal and the symbolic. My very literal dictionary, for instance, takes forty-two lines to define the reality of "love," but when I finished reading, I said, "That Noah Webster didn't know too much about love." On the other hand, a little girl's meticulously corn-rowed hair or a boy scrubbed and decked out for church "says" love, too, and in many ways far better than Mr. Webster.

Stories can tell important truths about human life without having literally, historically occurred. Folktales have been doing it for centuries: *Cinderella* tells the same truth as Our Lady's Magnificat, the lowly will be raised up; *Beauty and the Beast* says anything ugly, once it is loved, becomes beautiful; *Hansel and Gretel* shows (rather than tells) that sooner or later kids have to be booted from the nest and survive without parents. The whole *Star Wars* saga does the same thing; the Evil Empire doesn't exist; and yet it does; it always has. *Catcher in the Rye* never really happened, but it tells more about male adolescent psychology than any adolescent psychology book I've ever read—and I've been teaching male adolescents for nearly forty years.

Suppose you wanted to say something you found important about human life, like, "You know, it's not easy being an adolescent." No one could deny it, but . . . yawn. The plain old truth ends up pretty *blah*. So you change it to a metaphor: "Growing up isn't a single battle; it's a long, hard siege." Better, but there are so many other important things to say about the pains of growing up. So you decompact the metaphor into a story.

Once upon a time there was a young man named Youth who wanted very much to be a knight, sure of himself and his place in the world. His tutor, a wise but dithery old man named Merlin, described all the adventures he'd have to endure—the Forest of Despair, the Mountains of False Delight, the Swamp of Puberty where beautiful lilies and poisonous snakes abound. And on and on. But Youth was restless, so one day he set out with his squire, Hope, to rescue a damsel named Perfecta, locked away by the jealous witch, Time, guarded by the giant, Fear, who made up for an undeniable stupidity with a strength that could pop the heads of bulls like bottle caps. Along the way, Youth and Hope had many adventures, like skirmishes with packs of wolves from the Land of Doubt. . . .

And so on. You get the idea. That story never happened. (I know; I made it up.) But it does at least begin to tell a truth about growing up, more engaging than the literal truth and more detailed than the simple metaphor. Take it a bit further and you have the play *Everyman* or the novel *Pilgrim's Progress* or the folktale *Jack and the Beanstalk*. Change the simplistic names to Arthur, Lancelot, Mordred, and Morgan le Fey, and you have the Arthurian legends. Modernize it and put it in Philadelphia, and you have *Rocky*.

When Jesus taught, he almost invariably used the same method. He started with the truth he wanted to convey—not just offer but *impact* on the hearts of his listeners. "The Kingdom of

God is like a mustard seed . . . a banquet . . . a treasure found in a field." "A sower went out to sow his seed. . . . There was a father who had two sons. . . . Once there was a king who threw a banquet to celebrate his son's wedding." Perfectly obvious Jesus wasn't reporting literal history, that he'd actually witnessed a man beaten up on the road to Jericho and helped by a Samaritan or that he'd seen a shepherd leave ninety-nine sheep unguarded to go off after one stray. He could have, but it doesn't make any difference. He started with the truth—that we have to show compassion and that God values every single stray, and he made up the story to embody that truth.

The gospel writers and the early Church used exactly the same method. Take the angels at Bethlehem, for instance. Surely if the skies were ablaze with light and these great winged creatures were singing their (nonexistent) lungs out, somebody in the neighborhood besides a handful of shepherds would have *noticed*. How could Peter, James, and John have witnessed such an overpowering event as a literal transfiguration of Jesus and go back to being the same thick-headed pragmatists they'd been before?

The gospel writers were doing just what Jesus had done: Start with the truth, then find a story to capture it. Renaissance painters did the same thing. They weren't trying to depict what an eyewitness would have seen, with literalist eyes; they were trying to show what was *really* happening. This was an event superenergized by the transcendent presence of God.

We can't literally see that presence, just as we can't see electrons, or neutrinos, or the radio signals in this room, or the true selves of those whose bodies we can see. But they're there, just as the presence of God is. And the gospel writers and painters allow us to see what's really happening—like throwing clothes on the *Invisible Man*.

The story of feeding the five thousand starts with a literal truth: We all have a God-sized hunger. We can try to assuage that hunger with junk food—materialism, casual sex, primal scream, fame, domination—but they all leave us still wanting more. "Is that all there is?" As Augustine said, "Our hearts are restless till they rest in Thee." Anybody want to deny that truth? No one can. What this story is saying, I think, is that at the Last Supper Jesus *did* give us food that would fulfill that God-sized hunger, when he said, "This is my Body. . . . This is my blood." I can buy that, without having to necessarily say Jesus literally fed five thousand people.

At least for me, the only important miracle I have to take literally is the resurrection. I don't have to be troubled if Thomas didn't literally put his fingers in Jesus' wounds or Jesus didn't literally eat a piece of honeycomb. But as I hope to survive death myself, I have to trust that Jesus *did* defeat death and that—somehow—they experienced Christ truly risen, and they went to their deaths rather than deny it. Every one was a death-bed confession. I buy their testimony about that event, and after that all the other gospel miracles are negotiable—*because* of that one. I'm not denying they *could* have literally happened. (Who am I to tell God what he can and can't do?) But my faith in the gospels isn't threatened if they didn't. That experience of the risen Jesus justified all the stories they may have made up. At the transfiguration, the story exposed Jesus for who he truly was. And all the eyewitness cameras on earth couldn't have captured it.

Just as they did, I stake my life on it.

Questions to Ponder and Discuss

✤ In the *Constitution on Divine Revelation*, Vatican II urged ordinary Christians to frequent reading of Scripture, "for ignorance of the Scriptures is ignorance of Christ" (25). In what ways is that true? How is a person's faith and "connection" to

God impoverished if he or she relies solely on the rituals of the Mass, a half-grasped hearing of the readings once a week, and a homily which is sometimes "undependable"? One could almost call it a "secondhand" faith. Or is that being too harsh?

❧ These pages have often asked for a tolerance for ambiguity. How comfortable are you personally with an understanding of the Word of God in Scripture that is reassuring and yet incomplete, always open to a better understanding—like friendship, like marriage, like science? When I faced my faith crisis, discovering that Scripture was not as cut-and-dried as the Periodic Table, it helped me greatly to know that scholars who knew more about it than I did still said Mass every day. Believe it or not, that's still encouraging. "I believe. Help my unbelief."

❧ There are Christians who are wary of reading the Scriptures on their own, not because they are too busy or unintelligent but because their faith is both precious to them and fragile. They are afraid (as I was) that their faith might take a tailspin. But every growth in any faith relationship, as we have seen, involves a risk. Would it be worth the effort to find a very basic introduction to reading Scripture, perhaps even a high school or college text, to begin to explore the Bible without a teacher—as you must do in most other areas of your life? There are books too difficult for children, too simple for experts, but "just right" for educated persons who left learning about the faith long ago: *The Bible: NOW I Get It!*, by Gerhard Lohfink (Doubleday); *These Stones Will Shout*, by Mark Link (Thomas More); *Matthew, Mark, Luke, and You*, by William O'Malley (Thomas More).

❧ Just for yourself, try to figure out what the evangelist was trying to convey in the following statements. It might help to consult a scripture commentary in the library.

Whoever comes to me and does not hate father and mother, wife and children, yes, and even life itself, cannot be my disciple. (Luke 14:26)

Whoever loves his own life will lose it; whoever hates his own life in this world will keep it for life eternal.
(John 12:25)

Happy are those who mourn. (Matthew 5:4)

My soul magnifies the Lord. (Luke 1:46)

But when you give alms, do not let your left hand know what your right hand is doing. (Matthew 6:3)

Why, then, do you look at the speck in your brother's eye and pay no attention to the log in your own eye? (Matthew 7:3)

Truly, I tell you, whoever does not receive the Kingdom of God like a little child will never enter it. (Mark 10:15)

It was toward John that all the prophecies of the prophets and of the Law were leading, and he, if you will believe me, is the Elijah who was to return. (Matthew 7:14)

As they looked on, a change came over Jesus: his face was shining like the sun and his clothes were dazzling white. Then the three disciples saw Moses and Elijah talking with Jesus.
(Matthew 17:2-3)

Adam was a figure of the one who was to come. But the two are not the same, because God's free gift is not like Adam's sin.
(Romans 5:15)

❧ *Catechism:* 81, 101-141

❖ 10 ❖

THE HEBREW SCRIPTURES

The very heart of Christianity is inextricably rooted in what we have come to call, somewhat dismissively, the *Old* Testament. Jesus was a Jew, and his very soul was permeated by the beliefs, customs, and millennial history of his people. It would hardly be possible to understand the Christian Scriptures fully without some understanding of the Hebrew Scriptures, not only as the sole source of its allusions (like reading Shakespeare with no knowledge of mythology) but as the distillation of everything the Founder of Christianity took for granted about the reciprocal relationship between God and human beings. Again and again Jesus insists that what he says and does is "in fulfillment of the law and the prophets" (i.e., all the Hebrew Scriptures).

The Bible is not a scientific observation of human

history, nor were its authors ever troubled by speculative questions about the existence of Yahweh. That was simply a given. What was challenging for them was the human condition and human destiny before God. Their concerns were about God revealing himself in works of creating, providing, judging, rescuing, especially in his marriage covenant with his People and his promises for their deliverance through the ultimate Messiah ("Anointed One"). God is righteous, faithful, merciful, and loving. In contrast, the People are continually rebellious and alienated; the most consistent image for them is a wife who has deserted her ever-faithful husband and run to whoring after the pagan fertility gods (Baals). Nonetheless, Yahweh is by his very nature incapable of breaking his part of the covenant. Often, especially in the earlier books and in most of the prophets at the time when the Hebrews were farthest astray and when imminent retribution was obvious even to the most obtuse observer, Yahweh is described anthropomorphically as angry and vengeful (which God, of course, being perfect, could never be). But they also picture him standing humbly outside Israel's brothel, ready to take her back. "So I am going to take her into the desert again. There I will win her back with words of love. She will respond to me there as she did when she was young, when she came from Egypt. Then once again she will call me her husband. She will no longer call me her Baal" (Hosea 2:14-17). Quite simply: There is one God, and he cares for us.

The Hebrew Scriptures were, for the most part, the Jews' only library, a compilation of hero-stories combined with rules, anecdotes about kings, prophets, and priests, symbolic stories like Ruth, Esther, Jonah, collections of epigrams as in Proverbs, devotional poetry in the Psalms and erotic poetry in the Song of Songs, the elegy of Lamentations mourning over the fallen Jerusalem, the theological dialogue of Job, the oral addresses of the great prophets. The Bible ("The Book") maintained their identity as a

People, inspired their worship, pervaded their family life, sustained them in persecution, and ignited a devotion to intellectual pursuits from youth into old age.

Salvation History

It is history that provides the clue to understanding Judaism and Jews, for it was within space and time they engaged the Presence and found their identity as a people. Experience of the transcendent Yahweh in the here and now differentiates Jewish thought. Its devotion and moral uprightness root themselves in that experience, and in turn they serve as a model, the Suffering Servant, who calls all humankind to the same devotion and uprightness. "You only have I known of all the families of the earth; therefore I will punish you for all your iniquities" (Amos 3:1-3). With many variations in specifics, messianism has pervaded Jewish thinking for centuries and given the People a purpose, and the means to fulfill that purpose is codified in the Law.

There are eight major stages in the history of the People, the second four showing a rough parallel with the first four: (All dates in this chapter are B.C.)

The Patriarchs (ca. 19th c)

Kings and Prophets (1020-586)

Slavery in Egypt

Slavery in Babylon (586-538)

Exodus, Conquest of Canaan (13th c)

Return and Restoration (538-400)

Judges: Covenant community (1200-1020)

Subjugated religious community (3rd c to 3rd c C.E.)

The Patriarchs

The earliest stories in Hebrew history are of the Patriarchs: Abraham, Isaac, Jacob (whose name had been changed to *Israel*, "he wrestles with God"), and Jacob's twelve sons, most notably Joseph who became steward of the Egyptian Pharaoh. They are pictured as objects of Yahweh's particular care and personal concern; they responded in obedience and observance of sacrifice, particularly the ritual of male circumcision. Their ultimate destiny (eschatology) was God's promise of land and an endless posterity. The Lord took Abraham outside and said, "Look at the sky and try to count the stars. You will have as many descendants as that" (Genesis 15:5). In the stories of the patriarchs, there are none of the later struggles between Yahweh and Hebrews wandering off to pagan cults; rather, the emphasis is on family.

Slavery in Egypt

According to tradition, yet another famine occasioned a mass migration of twelve large Hebrew families looking for work and food in Egypt where eventually they were enslaved. In about the thirteenth century B.C., Yahweh raised up a charismatic leader named Moses who, with Yahweh's miraculous intervention by plagues and drowning of their enemies, led them out of bondage. There in the wilderness, at Mount Sinai, Yahweh made the Hebrews his people and offered them the terms of his Covenant, governing their conduct toward him and one another—not only within their nation but with all others, even aliens and slaves. In that Covenant, the Nation of Israel was born. Through a generation of wandering in the desert, Yahweh sustained them and finally led them to Canaan, the land promised to them since the days of Abraham.

It is impossible to negate a historical figure beneath whatever legendary accretions may have taken place in this story over the centuries. Like Mohammed, Moses was oracle, legislator, executive, and military strategist. He created most of the major institutions of Judaism: the priesthood and shrine, the Covenant and it commandments, the administration of what now became the Twelve Tribes of Israel. He was even credited with writing the five books of the Torah or Pentateuch, though that is hardly likely.

Conquest of Canaan

Although the stories of heroes (Judges) are also encrusted with legends (the sun standing still, the walls of Jericho collapsing at a blast of trumpets), archeological evidence does seem to give a solid underpinning to some of it. The tradition holds that the conquest of Canaan was a united effort of all the escaped Hebrews, aided by Hebrews who had remained behind, under the leadership of Moses' successor, Joshua. It was apparently a protracted affair, starting with an initial united assault; then individual tribes engaged in mopping-up operations for many years.

Judges were frequently local heroes (Gideon, Jephthah, Samson), and though they, too, are muffled with legends, their stories now seem substantially historical. A hallmark of Hebrew religion through the centuries has been a scrupulous avoidance of syncretism (absorbing new ideas and rites from other modes of thought: "Keep us from the strangers' ways.") But in this period Hebrews' assimilation of Canaanite religious ideas and practices (fertility rites, temple prostitutes both male and female) became an acute problem and would remain one for centuries. Moreover, they also suffered incursions from outside, particularly from the Philistines, equipped with new weapons of iron, who invaded the coast and established a league of five cities, then began to push further inland. (The land was later named after them: Palestine.)

This was to change the political identity of the People for quite some time. From the very beginning they had acknowledged no king but Yahweh. As Gideon says in Judges (8:23): "I will not rule you. My son will not rule you. Only Yahweh will." Almost surely, the Philistine threat precipitated them into a permanent political and military union under a single king. God-inspired judges were no longer enough; they needed a continuous central leadership to unite contrary factions and create a standing army.

Kings and Prophets

Saul was the first king; his successor was David, a former aide who had fallen out of favor with him. About 1010, he took over the rule of Judah in the south and ten years later the rule of Israel in the north. He established a truly centralized rule in Jerusalem, repelled foreign invaders, and created a new petty empire. He moved the Ark of the Covenant, containing the tablets of Sinai, to Jerusalem, and the entire "Hebrew" reality began to coalesce there. What emerged at this time was the conviction that from now on Yahweh would channel his benevolence to Israel through his anointed, some descendant of David.

Under David's son, Solomon, Israel became a thriving power; the city grew, including a splendid Temple. But Solomon gradually devolved from Solomon the Wise to merely Solomon the Magnificent. His large harem of wives, married in order to cement political alliances, brought with them foreign cults, each more appealing than bowing to an invisible Yahweh in an "empty" Temple. Prophets began to arise, and for generations would harass the kings for their apostasy. Solomon's oppressive policies, including forced labor in his building projects, incited defiance, and gradually the kingdom began to fall apart. The north became Israel, the south Judah.

There was great instability in the northern kingdom of Israel, owing at least partly to its separation from the unitive Temple in the south. For a relatively brief time (884-843), King Omri established order and prosperity, but in order to cement relations with the Phoenician kingdom of Tyre, he married his son, Ahab, to the Tyrian princess, Jezebel, who has become a byword for viciousness. Her attempt to spread the pagan cult aroused furious resistance from such ardent Yahwists as the prophets Elijah and his protege, Elisha, which ended in the slaughter of Jezebel and the whole royal family.

The rise of the Assyrian empire in the east gradually gobbled up the northern kingdom of Israel and reduced the southern kingdom of Judah to a vassal state. The fall of the northern kingdom was a major theme of the prophecies of Amos, Hosea, Isaiah, and Micah.

The southern kingdom enjoyed a precarious existence for another century and a half, due in part to the reforms of Hezekiah (715-686), returning to the worship of Yahweh. But under his successor, Manasseh (686-642), cults revived, even in the courtyards of the Temple. The people of Judah wavered back and forth between Yahwism and paganism. Under Josiah (640-609) another great reform took place as the power of Assyria began to wane, but gradually Babylon under King Nebuchadnezzar arose. For years, the prophet Jeremiah predicted the downfall of Judah, but no one listened. Finally, he told them their only hope was surrender. Josiah's son Zedekiah was furious and attempted to silence his "treachery," but in 586 Nebuchadnezzar finally broached the walls of Jerusalem, stripped anything of value, destroyed the Temple, and led off the nobility and all skilled artisans to slavery in Babylon.

Exile in Babylon

The scriptural themes now change from exhortation to lamentation but mixed with a stubborn hope as in Ezekiel and Second Isaiah (cc. 40-55 of Isaiah). The Hebrews in Babylon became more purely Yahwist than ever, clinging to the Sabbath and congregational prayer. In this period, they also began organizing the books of the Hebrew Scriptures. Finally, Cyrus the Great of Persia ("the Lord's Anointed") overcame Babylon and set the Hebrews free—50,000 men, women, and children, with 4,000 priests and 7,000 slaves.

Among the exiles in Babylon the prophet Ezekiel was haunted by memories of the defiled Temple and realized that, just as with the Flood, total destruction was necessary in order for the People to reconcile with Yahweh. Only through degradation could they be restored. Then Yahweh would breathe life into the dry bones of Israel and bring them back to life. Second Isaiah offered the same hope: Israel would rise again to be "a light for the nations, that Yahweh's salvation may reach to the end of the earth" (51:3). Though apparently lowly among the Gentiles, Israel would once again fulfill its messianic purpose.

Return and Restoration

The first great task upon their return (586) was the rebuilding of the Jerusalem Temple which had been the symbol of their unity as a people. It was completed in 515 and became the place of unbroken sacrifice for the next three and a half centuries. Reconstructing the Jerusalem walls became the task of Nehemiah, a Jew born in Babylon, who was appointed governor. He also began religious reforms, institutions that would make the Torah the very heart of Jewish life: observance of the Sabbath, fixed prayer and a pattern of annual fasts and feasts, gathering to study the Torah, and prohibition of marriage with non-Jews. The whole tone of the slowly healing restoration period was of repentance for their forebears' disloyalty to the Covenant with Yahweh. Ezra, a scholar and priest, brought the People once again into focus by reading to them "the book of the law of Moses" (probably Deuteronomy), bringing them back to strict observance, making the Torah not only the religious focus but the political law of the land. As the Law took root in the lives of the people, the spirit of the Law began to eclipse the spirit of the prophets who had tried so long and unsuccessfully to "keep us from the strangers' ways."

Subjugated Religious Community

With the exception of the brief period of the Maccabees, Israel would never again be a sovereign nation until the twentieth century. After 332, when they were conquered by Alexander the Great, the Jews began to face yet another incursion on their exclusivity, not the crude temptations of the Canaanite fertility cults but the more subtle temptation of *ideas*. The Bible was no longer the only book; it was only one of many books seducing the best minds to other ways of viewing human life. The Syrian occupiers forced Greek education (Hellenism) on all children. The prophet Sirach (also Ecclesiasticus, accepted by Roman Catholics, not by Jews and Protestants) wrote around 180 bitterly denouncing Hellenizers, offering instead personifications of virtues and vices, hypocrisy, generosity, filial respect, and especially Lady Wisdom, embodiment of the Law.

The conflict over the degree to which Jews should assimilate foreign ideas led to a civil war between those who advocated moderate Hellenism and those proposing total acculturation. The extremists appealed to the Syrian King Antiochus who intervened, promulgating decrees against all practice of Jewish religion, trying to force them into extinction, to the point of erecting a statue of Zeus in the center of the Temple (cf. book of Daniel). This in turn provoked a revolt of ardent Yahwists (Hasideans) under the priest Mattathias and his five sons, the so-called Maccabees, who adamantly refused to conduct or participate in pagan rituals. The power of the Hellenizers lay mostly among the wealthy, while the broader influence of the Maccabees lay among the peasants and urban masses. Mattathias's eldest son, Judas, proved a military genius, defeating four Syrian armies. In December 164, he succeeded in tearing down the statue of Zeus and forcing the new Syrian king to allow Israel's independence—which lasted for nearly a century. Jews celebrate that event yearly at Hanukkah ("Dedication") or the Feast of Lights.

In 63, the Romans conquered Palestine and instituted puppet kings, all devoted to Rome and Hellenistic ways. In 37, Herod the Great became king who, though a practicing Jew, was Arab on both sides. He rebuilt the Temple, Greek theaters, amphitheaters, and racecourses. Herod had a dark and sinister streak and grew more mentally unstable as he grew older. The slaughter of the innocents in Bethlehem at the birth of a rumored messiah was quite within his capability. After an unsuccessful suicide attempt, Herod died, and Palestine was divided among his sons, Archelaus in Judea, Philip in Samaria, and Herod in Galilee.

It was, as the old Martyrology for Christmas sang, "the fullness of time." The world had been prepared for The One Who Is to Come.

146 WILLIAM J. O'MALLEY

Questions to Ponder and Discuss

✦ It is, of course, impossible to sum up the history of a people of such great faith in just a few pages, impossible to catch anything but the slightest hint of the spirit that energizes them and the history in which they still ground that faith and spirit. But reflect on those hints: their absolute conviction of the caring providence of God, their honest confrontation with their own sinfulness, the conviction of their purpose in God's plan as the scapegoat for "the nations," the resilience which is a hallmark of their identity from the Exodus through the Holocaust, the continuing pattern of Covenant, wandering from it, the resulting devastation and alienation, and returning to begin the slow process of starting all over, yet again. How can the experience of this holy People, which was part and parcel of Jesus' human character, enrich your experience as part of a new holy People? How can their faith and spirit enliven your faith and spirit?

✦ The Yiddish word *nebbish* means a drab, insignificant person who is generally ignored. And if you read the Hebrew Scriptures carefully (trying to uproot the totally untrue impression of biblical characters from Hollywood epics about them), Yahweh shows an unarguable preference for nebbishes—dweebs, klutzes, losers. Adam and Eve had messed up the Eden experiment, but he starts over again with the *same* pair of bunglers. Noah was a drunk with a quite eccentric family. In order to start a nation as numerous as the stars in the sky, Yahweh goes to Abram and Sarai, both in their nineties and barren as a pair of bricks. The Moses you find in the Bible is in no way like the Moses in the *Ten Commandments*. He stammered, and tried for two or three pages to weasel out of the job; far more like Don Knotts than like Charlton Heston. (Cecil B. DeMille rewrote the scenario perhaps the way God would have written it). Yahweh wants to bring down a giant named Goliath, so he sends Samuel to a family of herculean brothers only to dismiss them all and pick David, the spindly kid with a slingshot. After awhile, the pattern seems inescapable: God loves a nebbish. What does that say about what God can do with you, if you're willing? What does the way God treated a clumsy, self-centered, materialist Israel tell us about what God can do with a polarized, fractious, at-odds-with-itself Church today?

✤ The reforms throughout the history of the Jews, no matter how intense for a while, seemed always short-lived—at least until the one following the Babylonian Exile, which seems to have lasted for a good many Jews to this very day. What was different about that post-Exilic reform, arising as it did not out of speculation and meditation but out of degradation? Does it say anything about our own personal conversions? Does it offer any advice for the reforms on the Church?

✤ Scripture: Matthew 5:16-18; Mark 9:2-13; Luke 24:43-45

✤ *Catechism:* 436-440, 539, 674, 759-762, 839-840

As society is now constituted, a literal adherence to the moral precepts scattered throughout the Gospels would mean sudden death.

—Alfred North Whitehead, *Adventures in Ideas*

❊ 11 ❊

THE GOSPEL BECOMES THE GOSPELS

There is a true and important difference between "historical" and "historic." "Historical" means the actual event, what people present at the time witnessed; "historic" means the event-as-interpreted: what it means in the whole perspective of human life and human significance. During the Civil War, for instance, a great many men on both sides fought and died at Gettysburg. There was audible gunfire; individual men stood on specific spots; specific persons died here and over there and up there. It was historical; it actually happened. But it was just one more battle, one more occurrence, until Abraham Lincoln *interpreted* it, put it into the whole perspective of what the war was all about and what human dignity is all about. In a very real sense, the reason we remember what men did at Gettysburg is what Lincoln *said* there. The historical event became historic when Lincoln showed its meaning. So, too, the work of the gospel writers.

The gospels aren't biographies; they're a *message*. If you want the bare-bones truth, you can find it in Saint Paul:

First and foremost, I handed on to you the facts which had been imparted to me: That Christ died for our sins, in accordance with the Scripture, that he was buried, that he was raised to life on the third day, according to the Scriptures, and that he appeared to Cephas [Peter] and afterward to the Twelve and in the end, he appeared even to me (I Corinthians 15:3-8).

That's it; bare bones.

Every weekend, the homilist struggles to decompact that basic set of truths, given his own talents and limitations, given the teachers who have opened up or frozen his mind: Who was this person Jesus; what did his speaking and actions attempt to say about us and God; how should this event change our lives, our minds, our attitudes two thousand years later? In the same way, the gospel writers spoke of Jesus as he actually was (historical) but also of what Jesus *meant* (historic). These evangelists were not professional historians; they were homilists—trying to change minds.

There is only *one* true test of the gospels. It isn't found in the most scrupulous examination of the validity of the texts. It isn't found in the rock-solid declarations of the Church. The trustworthiness of the gospels emerges when what they say about human life *works*. That's why I believe Claire Booth Luce's test is the true one: "Can I see your freedom? Can I feel your joy?" Surely, *that* is what accounted for the flood of conversions in the early Church: these Christians were unarguably *happy!* Their lives—even their sufferings—made *sense* to them.

Recall what we said at the beginning about the faith in friendship and marriage. The relationship grows only when one trusts the other *before* the other has "proven" his or herself worthy of that trust. The proof comes after the trust has been given and validated. The same is true of the gospels. If you start out from disbelief, you might as well be deciphering the memorabilia of Bantus or Mayans. But if a reader accepts the resurrection, it changes radically his or her understanding of the gospels' words and actions and events. For the nonbeliever, reading the Scriptures is like eavesdropping on a conversation between friends. For the believer, it is like being in on the conversation as one of the friends.

The same was true for these writers. Each one wrote not only as a believer, but as an *individual* believer, with a unique mind-set, personality, attitude, dominant concerns, and specific audience. Just as a viewer can tell a difference between the temperaments of Rembrandt and Picasso sheerly by studying their work, so we can tell the difference between the individuals who wrote First Isaiah and Second Isaiah. Just so, we can also tell the difference between Mark, Matthew, Luke, and John.

Mark was the first written life of Jesus. It is the briefest, with a severe outline and rugged style, spare and without embellishments, almost rough. For instance, though most translations render Jesus' order to the storm at sea as "Be calm" or "Be still," Mark's Greek verb is much closer to our "Shut *up!*" Mark, who was quite likely Peter's interpreter in Rome, was writing under pressure, without the time to indulge himself in Matthew's anchoring the message in quotes from the Old Testament, or Luke's elegant style, or John's mystical theologizing. His style is almost childish, breathless, rushed: "And then they. . . . and then he . . . and then." Mark is writing for non-Jews, which is evident in the fact that he translates Hebrew terms. He shows Jesus slowly revealing the "messianic secret" of his true identity, and he very frequently describes Jesus curing physical blindness, symbolic of soul-blindness. Mark's Jesus reveals himself slowly in climactic moments: first, Peter's recognition of him as messiah (8:29); second, Jesus' reply to the high priest that he is indeed "the Son of the Blessed One" (14:62), and finally, the climax of his whole gospel when the pagan Roman centurion declares, "Truly, this was the Son of God!" (15:29).

Matthew addresses a Jewish-convert audience different from Mark's. His gospel is filled with quotations and allusions to the Hebrew Scriptures in an attempt to prove Jesus is truly their fulfillment: the Messiah, and the new Christian community is the new Chosen People. He wrote after the Jewish revolt had provoked the Romans to destroy Jerusalem and the Temple and had dispersed a great many of its inhabitants out into the far-flung reaches of the Empire. Judaism, at least as far as they knew it, had ended, and a new life had begun. Despite his legal background, Matthew is the most antipharisaic of the evangelists, as was Paul, the converted pharisee. His twenty-third chapter is a textbook of vilification against them. (Think of a reformed smoker.) Matthew's five discourses purposely mirror the five books of the Torah, showing Jesus is the new Moses, the long-promised suffering servant of Yahweh. First, a discourse on discipleship (the Sermon on the Mount); second, on apostleship and spreading the Good News; third, parables of the new Kingdom; fourth, on community administration; fifth, on the fulfillment of the Kingdom in heaven. Finally, as in all four gospels, the Passion and resurrection seal the message.

Luke and *Acts* were undoubtedly a dual work written by the same writer, both dedicated to "Theophilus." It is a sweeping study first of Jesus, ending in a sole journey to Jerusalem, then of Peter, Paul, and the early community, ending in Rome, the center of the known world. Not only is Luke an elegant stylist, but a sensitive human soul. Only he gives the table talk, the friendliness, the great parables of human kindness (Good Samaritan, Prodigal Son, Rich Man and Lazarus, Zaccheus,

Good Thief, the disciples on the road to Emmaus). Only Luke
tones down the harshness of Jesus' treatment during the Passion,
almost as if he couldn't bring himself to picture such a Person so
humiliated. He takes great pains to show there was nothing polit-
ically subversive or socially revolutionary about the new
movement. He writes primarily for Gentiles, and the graceful
Greek suggests a more learned audience. He avoids Aramaic
words common to Matthew, like "rabbi" or "Abba." Instead, he
calls Jesus "Teacher" or "Master."

John follows, in broad outlines, the same general sequence as
the other three, from Jesus' origins to his crucifixion, but his
scope is far more otherworldly than this-worldly, philosophical,
"spiritual." His was surely the last gospel written; it presumes
knowledge of the Twelve, and therefore doesn't mention their
calling, nor does it mention Jesus' baptism or show a clear institution of the Eucharist. John shows no exorcisms, no parables,
no simple moral instructions, no debates about the Law. He
presumes not only the basic tradition but sixty years of reflection
on it. His main emphasis is on Jesus' preaching, in far longer
sessions than in the other three gospels, giving a more
profoundly theological vision of *the Christ* rather than "merely"
the historical Jesus. John's Jesus is much closer to the Jesus of the
great Eastern Orthodox mosaics than to "realistic" pictures of a
life-sized, earthly human being.

Since both Matthew and Luke reproduce nearly all of Mark's
gospel, often verbatim, it is clear each had a copy of Mark and
wrote a "new edition" of Mark when new sources became
available. (John's approach is so unique we will have to leave him
aside to concentrate on the three with more closely similar
outlines.) The gospels of Mark, Matthew, and Luke are called
"synoptic," from the Greek word *synoptikos,* "seeing the whole
thing together." It is the same root as for "synopsis." They yield
up so many more insights when one places them in parallel

columns (see Throckmorton, *Gospel Parallels*) and understands that each of these unique writers acted not only as *collectors* of materials but also as highly individual *editors* or interpreters of it.

The Composition of the Gospels

The Evangelists as Collectors. The first written form of the gospel message was not the gospels but the letters of Saint Paul, written in the fifties and sixties. Most scripture scholars agree Mark was written in about 65, Matthew and Luke-Acts in the mid-70s, and John in the 90s. If Jesus died in the mid-30s, why did they wait so long to get the message onto paper, where it could endure?

In the first place, once again, we have to remember we are dealing with a totally different culture, not like our own with instant reportage and commentary, with the world spilling into everyone's living room at six and eleven every evening. It was weeks before people in Galilee even heard rumors of what was transpiring in Jerusalem. Further, although there were libraries in the great metropolitan centers, by far the majority of the people in the Roman Empire couldn't read. Theirs was a much more oral culture, news passed by word of mouth. There was very little value in writing down the gospel message when very few potential converts could even read it.

However, because of that illiteracy, ordinary people developed far better memories than ours, which is one reason scholars suspect the core of the beatitudes (which depend on a formula) and the parables (which are in story form) are the closest we have to accurate recollections of Jesus' actual words. Hard to imagine the life of the earliest listeners to the gospels, undistracted by a glut of television, newspapers, magazines, and billboards. They had a small—and therefore easily learned—body of literature in the Hebrew Scriptures, less than a thousand pages, which was their sole library of religion, culture, and entertainment. They heard it read again and again in the synagogue; children memorized long passages at the behest of rabbi-teachers. When you have nothing else to do with your spare time, whether it be whittling or retelling stories, you tend to become rather good at it.

The most important reason for the delay in writing it all down was the fact that most early Christians believed the End was at hand. It hardly seems profitable to write history when you believe history is about to end. Paul wrote letters, not because he hoped they would be preserved for many generations, but because he was doing exactly the work of the Gospel—interpreting the message of Jesus to particular audiences and their particular problems at the moment. His interpretations were written simply because he was in one place and his audience was in another. He almost certainly never dreamed he was writing "Scripture."

Most likely, many of the oral communications about the life and words of Jesus were gradually put together in small written collections centered around a common theme: poverty and riches, seed parables, various beatitudes, statements various witnesses recalled Jesus making (probably many repetitions in different places)—all brought together in little scrolls, for the convenience of preachers and catechists. Finally, Mark collected such booklets, combined them and arranged them into a full (for the moment) treatment of the life and message of Jesus.

Basically, there are four reasons for finally resorting to writing. First, the End didn't literally happen; they had to go back and re-think what Jesus must have meant. Gradually, they began to realize he meant the end of life *as they knew it;* that the Kingdom was spiritual, not literal. Second, the original eyewitnesses were dying out, and it was essential to preserve their testimony. Third, there was just the natural inclination to reflect and probe more deeply into the meaning of the personality and message of the most important Person in human history. Finally, as the Church spread into the Greco-Roman world, the message became subject to influences from all kinds of foreign religions and philosophical movements. Thus, it was in danger of being adapted and reinterpreted in ways different from—or even contrary to—Jesus' original intention and the experience of the first apostolic witnesses. The Church does the same still today, testing new insights against the recorded intentions of its founder.

Form criticism—studying the evangelists as *collectors*—is a highly technical, scholarly, scientific study of the linguistic forms of the Greek New Testament. It tries to discern beneath unusual Greek sentence structures the original Aramaic in which Jesus or the earliest community stated the original orally. It also studies additions to the original—like experts peeling away one layer of paint after another to get down to the original work. This can be determined, for instance, by customs which came later than the time of Jesus or were proper to cultures outside Palestine. Further, they study concerns described as if brought to Jesus but which did not actually arise until after his death, like Jewish birth families turning in Christian-convert relatives to the synagogue. Scholars can also discern passages whose formulation looks as if they have been drawn up for liturgical purposes in the early community or as handbooks for new converts.

The first written gospel was Mark's, and he appears to have three sources: first, Peter himself, whose interpreter he apparently was; second, a passion narrative previously written which Mark takes almost "whole," the style being somewhat unlike his usual; and third, for want of a better term, "other sources," small collections of sayings, stories picked up from recent emigrés from Palestine to Rome. Therefore, Mark is the primary source for the other two synoptics. They recopy almost all of Mark's gospel.

Patterns begin to emerge. For instance, wherever the three synoptics agree almost exactly, it is the order of Mark, the first written gospel. Matthew's and Mark's versions may agree "against" Luke's, but Matthew and Luke never agree together "against" Mark. They may have material (about 250 verses) Mark does not have at all but which is verbally identical in Luke and Matthew, from a common source both Luke and Matthew had but Mark did not (which scholars call "Q" from the German word *Quelle,* meaning "source").

Beyond that, Matthew and Luke each have material that is not found in the other gospel version nor in Mark, material exclusive to that particular gospel. Thus, scholars postulate a source (or sources) for Matthew called "M" with material unknown to either Mark or Luke and a source (or sources) for Luke called "L" with material unknown to either Mark or Matthew.

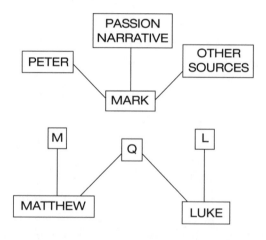

The Evangelists as Editors. Take an analogy to a news program like *60 Minutes.* The people in charge claim to be as objective as they can. But it is obvious their choice of which programs to air and which ones to scrap indicates a particular state of mind, a set of priorities in values—not merely governed by viewers' interests but also by the staff's judgment of the subject's objective importance. What's more, like lawyers, they are making a *case,* trying to show that this car company or that tobacco company is bilking customers. And over a generation, they have proven themselves capable and trustworthy. They *collect* and *edit.* So, too, the gospel writers.

Therefore, if one of the evangelists diverges from the others in his choice of words, or changes the audience or setting for a speech of Jesus, or puts a particular event in a different place in his overall narrative, the choice is motivated by the writer's conviction that some nuance or facet of the basic message will be better served by his placement—whether or not the event historically occurred then and there or not. Similarly, any speaker would change his or her "tack" speaking to eight retired nuns from what he or she might opt for with eight hundred high-school boys.

This will be clearer if we consider a passage from the Passion (where the synoptics are most alike) and show how and why they differ. When you read them in parallel, begin with *Mark*, the original. *Luke* is on the next page. Underline where they are nearly verbally identical; draw a broken line under words and phrases more or less the same; box in places only one of the three has an entry.

Mark 15	Matthew 27	Luke 23
And the curtain of the temple was torn in two from top to bottom.	And behold, the curtain of the temple was torn in two, from the top to bottom; and the earth shook and the rocks were split. The tombs were also opened and many bodies of the saints who had fallen asleep were raised. And coming out of the tombs after his resurrection, they went into the holy city and appeared to many.	[See verse 45.]
And when the centurion who stood facing him saw that he thus breathed his last, he said, "Truly this man was the Son of God!"	When the centurion and those who were with him, keeping watch over Jesus, saw the earthquake and what took place, they were filled with awe and said, "Truly this was the Son of God!"	Now when the centurion saw what had taken place, he praised God and said, "Certainly this man was innocent." And all the multitudes who assembled to see the sight, when they saw what had taken place, returned home, beating their breasts.

It is obvious all three have *similarities*. They are all speaking of the same historical event: the death of Jesus. The three have common details: the centurion and the people and their reactions to Jesus' death. But there are *differences*:

Luke has put the detail of the torn curtain earlier, in his verse 45, *before* Jesus died. The moment itself is probably only symbolic rather than a historical event. This curtain hung in front of the Holy of Holies, the most sacred place in the Jewish cult. But why does Luke put it before Jesus' death rather than where it was in his copy of Mark? Probably to say in symbolic terms that it was Judaism which was defeated at this moment and not Jesus.

Matthew is the Steven Spielberg of the gospel writers. He likes special effects to underline significance: an earthquake, tombs opening and yielding up their dead, and Hebrew saints coming to life again after the resurrection of Jesus. The earthquake (which the Hebrew Scriptures said figuratively were the steps of Yahweh passing) is a sign that says God is leaving Israel behind. Also, it is surely one of the signs of the beginning of the End when the remnant of Israel will be freed. Through the symbol of the risen dead, Matthew can connect the resurrection of the believer with the resurrection of Jesus. That is why the Messiah had to die. Matthew is writing for a Jewish audience who would grasp these allusions more readily than Gentiles.

Note carefully the declaration after Jesus' death. Mark, writing primarily for Gentiles, has this supreme declaration of his gospel come from the lips of a Gentile Roman. Matthew, writing for Jews, says the testimony comes also from "those who were with him," other Roman soldiers who testified in words the Jews of Jesus couldn't use and so that, legally, there was more than one witness. Moreover, the holy Jewish dead also testified to Jesus' divinity by their "rising." Luke, writing for an educated Greco-Roman audience, has the official Roman witness, the centurion, declare that he was certainly innocent, i.e., not guilty of any crime against the Roman state. And the "multitudes," the Jews, return to their homes acknowledging their guilt.

Each of the three tells of the same event, but each from a different point of view, for a different audience and with a different purpose. Historically, who knows what the people who actually stood at the cross thought or said? The point is that Jesus actually did die, and that event and its aftermath, the resurrection, called for a response.

This consideration of how the Gospel became the gospels might seem at first overly complex and scholarly. Actually, it was intended at least to suggest that there is not that much to worry about regarding the validity of the gospel message. As I said when I described the tailspin my earliest scripture courses caused, what kept me going was that the scripture professors—who knew far more than I—still offered Mass each morning. Whenever you feel confused about a particular segment of the gospels, there are commentaries aplenty, ranging from the highly technical to the easily accessible, written by women and men who know more clearly what the original writers intended. You can *know*—and still *believe*.

In reading Scripture, as in reading Shakespeare, there is a place for both head and heart. One can analyze, dissect, probe logical relationships as a critic would—and the text will yield up far more than it ever has before. But, analysis done, one must go back and reread the text with completely different powers of the soul—imagination, emotion, love, spirit—not as a critic but as a poet. Otherwise, one is left after the analysis with the various parts of a corpse. Analysis reveals hidden parts, but only imagination can reenliven them.

Questions to Ponder and Discuss

❧ The Jesus we find in the gospels never said anything about atomic war, artificial birth control, genetic engineering. How do we apply the core of Jesus' message to those problems which didn't exist in Jesus' lifetime—just as the early Church did with the torments of the arena, the dispersal of Israel, the struggle between Christian community and synagogue? How do we apply his convictions to issues which existed at his time, like abortion and homosexuality, but which he never explicitly discussed—or at least is not reported as having discussed them?

❧ How much does it bother you (if at all) that the gospels are not PBS documentaries? Since the assassination of Jack Kennedy and all that followed, I suspect we are more cautious about being hoaxed than any other society in history. Any world where the *National Enquirer* is taken even half seriously and sometimes quoted in the legitimate press is going to have a tough time generating heroes or heroines. But start your investigation of the gospels not from skepticism but from susceptibility, from the position that says, "Okay, *what if* Jesus really was who he claimed to be?" Let's just say, for the moment, for the sake of argument, that what the gospels say about him is substantially true—the core message. How ought that to change my life? Accepting that, again at least for the moment, why not try it and see if it works?

❧ When you visit Rome as a tourist, you can enter the Forum and say, "Julius Caesar and Saint Paul actually stood on these very stones." On the contrary, when you visit Palestine, all the places Jesus stood are fifteen meters below the surface—or some pious group has heaped up a great cathedral over the spot. When I was in Bethlehem, the guide pointed to a place enclosed like a fireplace with a big golden starburst embedded in the floor. He said, "This. Birthplace of Jesu Chreest!" I asked, "How sure are they?" He gave me a huge Semitic shrug. Granted that it would be a support to faith to be able to say, even with some semblance of certainty, "Yes. We know that Jesus actually stood here on this stone." But does it really matter?

❧ The *Catechism* states: "The Paschal mystery of Christ's cross and Resurrection stands at the center of the Good News that the apostles, and the Church following them, are to proclaim to the world. God's saving plan was accomplished 'once for all' by the redemptive death of his Son Jesus Christ" (571). If you can "buy" the resurrection, what more do you need?

❧ The ultimate test of the gospels is not whether Jesus gave the sermon on the mount on this particular hill (as Matthew has it) or on a plain (as Luke has it). Jesus himself said, "By their *fruits* you will know them." When people act *as if* what Jesus said and did is true, does it change their *lives?* We're not talking about those who merely give lip service to the gospel, but those who genuinely believe it in their heart-of-hearts. Does it make them more open-minded, openhearted, openhanded? Are they more forgiving, as Jesus was with "the woman known as a sinner in the town," the adulterous woman, the Samaritan woman at the well, the prodigal son, the repentant Peter? Do they treat "the least of my brethren" as they would treat Jesus come back? Do they face tragedy with the same trusting equanimity Jesus faced it in his Passion?

❧ *Catechism:* 81, 124-141 (Jerome Biblical Commentary)

*About Jesus and the Church, I simply know
they're just one thing, and we shouldn't
complicate the matter.*

—Saint Joan of Arc

✳ 12 ✳

THE CHURCH

As we saw earlier, the *images* we have of Yahweh and of
Jesus are influenced far more by middling Church art
and untrue biblical movies than by studying the Hebrew
or Christian Scriptures and pondering what they mean.
Our image of the Church seems also skewed. What
comes to mind when you think of the word "church" in
statements like, "When is the Church going to do
something about . . . ," is ordinarily the *official* Church,
the Vatican. "Them" as distinguished from "us." Some
women rightly object that they have no opportunity for
ministerial power in "the Church," but fail to realize that
by far most Catholic males lack access to that same
power. Rarely does anyone seem to mean by "church"
what the early disciples who died for it meant by the
word.

When Jesus tried to explain the Kingdom of God, he always resorted to analogies, and there are many (overlapping) images which give us a much less reductionist understanding than the Church as institution. (cf. Dulles, *Models of the Church* and *Catechism* 748-862) Some give insight into the Church as a unique entity within itself, and others give insight into the Church in contact with the world outside it. ("Who are we?" and "Where do we fit in?")

From the start, I confess a certain bias against two of them, despite their evident use in Scripture and throughout the history of the Church. I feel less than comfortable with the Church as a sheepfold or the attendant idea that bishops carry shepherds' crooks and the local clergy are called "pastors." Perhaps it's something persnickety and unredeemed (or American) in me, but I don't think God made me to be a witless, tractable sheep. True, in regard to Jesus, I am a child or sheep, but in regard to the world, I'm convinced God wants me to be an adult and a shepherd myself. I respect and value advice from the hierarchy, but I think God also gave intelligence to the rest of us for some reason. The other image I balk from is the Church as a temple built of living stones, of which Jesus is the essential cornerstone. The combination of dull and inert stone with energizing life eludes my imagination.

The other images, though, I find helpful: those about the Church's self-identity (People of God, Body of Christ, Bride) and those about the Church's purpose outside itself (Sacrament, Herald, Servant), and finally, inevitably, the Church as Institution.

The Church as a Community

The People of God. God is not the exclusive property of any individual group of people or any cult, but just as the Hebrews believed Yahweh, through Moses, chose Israel to be his special covenanted people, Christians believe God, through Jesus Christ, invites us to be the new "messianic people." Whatever can be said about the Jews as God's Chosen can now be said of us. Like Israel we are the bride of God; the two—the God-Man and the Church—will be one flesh and no longer two. As Joan of Arc said, "They're just one thing." Others are always welcome, and our calling is no denigration of their honest goodness. They simply never heard the invitation or have chosen not to accept it.

In Acts, Saint Peter said, "I now realize that it is true that God treats everyone on the same basis. Whoever fears him and does what is right is acceptable to him" (10:34). Nor should anyone suffer compulsion to accept the Church. Vatican II's *Declaration on Religious Freedom* is quite clear: "This freedom means that all [human beings] are to be immune from coercion on the part of individuals or of social groups and of any human power, in such wise that in matters religious no one is to be forced to act in a matter contrary to his [or her] own beliefs" (2).

The Greek word for the Church is *ekklesia,* "those who are called out." Just as Yahweh summoned Abraham out of Ur of the Chaldees, and the Hebrew slaves from the camps of Egypt, and the exiles from bondage in Babylon, we are summoned from the world and then sent back into the world. The root of the English word "Church" is the Greek *Kyriake* and the German *Kirche:* "what belongs to the Lord," and it applies to the church building and the local community within it, to the whole web of relationships spreading out across the face of the globe—and even beyond it, into the communion of saints in heaven, and into the inner life of the Holy Trinity.

The Body of Christ

As the *Catechism* puts it, "Not only is [the Church] gathered *around* [Christ]; she is united in him, *into his* body" (789). The risen Jesus is the head of this mystical body, the Holy Spirit is its enlivening soul, and we—as diverse as the members of any body—are its members. Just as Eve was born from the side of the sleeping Adam, the Church was born from the pierced side of Christ dying on the cross. Jesus gives a similar analogy: "I am the vine; you are the branches. Whoever remains in me, and I in him, will bear much fruit" (John 15:5). The life of the Trinity pulses in our souls and our assemblage; we are the adopted members of their royal family, peers of their Realm.

We are a living organism, unified in our diversity. On the one hand, our differences don't really count. As Saint Paul says, "So there is no difference between Jews and Gentiles, between slaves and free, between men and women; you are all one in union with Christ Jesus" (Galatians 3:28). On the other hand, our differences are a distinct advantage; each of us has a unique contribution to make of which the others are incapable: "So then, the eye cannot say to the hand, 'I don't need you!' Nor can the head say to the feet, 'Well, I don't need you!'" (I Corinthians 12:21). As we shall see, the cab driver and the beautician can reach out to people even the pope cannot touch.

Our incorporation ("in-body-ment") into Christ begins in baptism, when we are plunged into the waters of his death and emerge into his superenergized new life, and it renews itself whenever we receive the Eucharist, taking the life of God into ourselves again. "For my flesh is the real food; my blood is the real drink. Whoever eats my flesh and drinks my blood lives in me, and I live in them" (John 6:56).

On the one hand, to anyone who believes what we can see limits what can be real, such explanations are meaningless. On the other, trying to box that reality more precisely is like trying to lasso the wind. Joan of Arc put it with magnificent peasant simplicity: "About Jesus and the Church, I simply know they're just one thing, and we shouldn't complicate the matter." *Brava!*

The Church as Messiah

Sacrament. Any sacrament is a visible sign of an invisible reality, a real-if-unseen transformation, as in a wedding. Just as Israel was a sign of Yahweh's saving presence among the nations, and Jesus was the sacrament of God's infusion into humankind, so the Church is a cohesive unity that embodies that Presence and mediates it outward into the world. That mission is captured in the title of one of the major essays of Vatican II, *Lumen Gentium,* "the light of all peoples."

Like John the Baptist, we are sent as a herald to "make straight the way of the Lord," to make the Gospel at least a bit less inaccessible. Our mission is to be the salt of the earth and the light of the world. There is no room for shyness here. We are to get up on the housetops and shout the Good News: We need never fear death or meaninglessness, and there is no sin beyond forgiveness. On the orders of Jesus himself, we are sent out there to *shine!*

Servant

Jesus "emptied himself" and took on the nature of a slave, to show us how it's done.

At the Last Supper, before he instituted the sacrament of the Eucharist, he made another sacramental gesture to indicate the Church's mission. He removed his outer clothing, got down on his knees, and washed the feet of his disciples. "I, your Teacher and Lord, have just washed your feet. You, then, should wash one another's feet. I have set an example for you, so that you will do just what I have done for you" (John 13:14-15). Then Jesus literally broke himself up and passed round the pieces. He came not to be served, but to serve.

Countless men and women who have no connection with the Church selflessly and nobly serve the needy. What the members of the Church add when they offer the same compassion is to serve not only a brother or sister in anguish but also, by that same act, to serve the Christ lurking within each one. "Whenever you did it to the least of mine, you did it to me" (Matthew 25:40).

Pilgrim

Before, I said one of the best images I knew of the Church was the Barque of Peter. This image is apt because it captures the fact we are on a journey, together; we haven't arrived, and until death or the end of the world (whichever comes first), we will not "arrive." We will always be wayfarers, on the move, without certainty and surely without perfection. Meanwhile, we live and work with a reality which is often quite distant from the rosy ideals we have considered so far.

"Homilies are twenty minutes of detours. . . . They keep bringing in new hymns we don't know. . . . The pastor can be very . . . well, condescending." The question in reply: Then what are we—the Church—going to *do* about that? "Why can't women and married men be priests? Why is 'the Church' so hung up on sex? Do you mean artificial birth control between two committed people is as bad a mortal sin as infanticide or slavery?" The only "answer" I know is Reinhold Niebuhr's prayer: *God, grant me the serenity to accept the things that* [for now] *can't be changed; the courage to change the things that can be changed; and the wisdom to know the difference.*

As with all ideals, the images we have seen of the Church are like the North Star—guides, not a destination. We are on a pilgrimage, together, and like the Hebrews in the desert, there is no end of muttering and grumbling. We have different spiky agendas, different ideas about what is crucial, different attitudes toward authority. But we still do agree on the nonnegotiables:

168 WILLIAM J. O'MALLEY

the incarnation, the resurrection, the importance of the spiritual and eternal over the material and temporal, the worshiping and serving community. Our journey is to make human living better, not perfect. And, in the going, we're already "there."

The Church as Institution

Several years ago, a group of students wanted to start a lacrosse team, but no faculty member wanted to be the moderator or coach. "Well, we'll just get together and do it ourselves." It lasted about a week: "I've got a dentist appointment. How come you never play me? Who says you can tell me what to do?" I've directed about fifty musicals, and there is no way I could put thirty dancers on a stage—no matter how willing, tireless, or talented—and have them "just come up with" the danceoff in the gym of *West Side Story* without any kind of authoritative *direction*. The predictability of the universe and the progression of evolution prove you can't get regularity out of an accident or order out of luck. Even truer working with human beings who, unlike planets and platypuses, have free will. We all agree we can get more done together, sharing our complementary talents, compromising with less than perfection, than we can working in isolation. But in order to do that, we have to yield to an awareness of original sin. If everybody grabs the tiller, the Barque of Peter will end up sailing in circles. We need a captain, and the captain needs officers, and the officers need petty officers, and—no matter what anybody thinks—none of the higher-ups is going to get anywhere without the regular crew: us.

The Hierarchy and Clergy

I don't know why we always start here, but we do. Perhaps because the hierarchy is an aspect of the Roman Catholic Church which no other group has, to the point that it is constitutive. But the pope, the bishops, and the officials of the Roman curia are not "more Catholic" than you or I. They just fulfill a different function. Those who exercise sacramental and governmental ministry in the Church realize that the root of the word "minister" is to serve, to advise. They are, in fact, "the servants of the servants of God." Although there are some who complain that these servants spend too much time fussing about internal housekeeping details and too little on evangelization, most bishops know they are not merely builders and watchdogs of orthodoxy, but are meant to enliven, enable, empower the Church—us—to serve better.

It is incontestable that Jesus singled out Peter to be "the rock" *on* which he was founding the Church, to serve a unifying and governing power no other apostle shared alone without Peter. Whether those words come from Jesus himself or from the early Church, they have as much reliability as the rest of the most ancient Christian Scriptures. And no matter how historians might quibble over the purity of the apostolic succession of popes since then, we can trust that it is "more or less" a reliable sequence, and it is equally incontestable that for centuries, in the Roman Church, the pope has always been the Vicar of Christ. If you don't accept that, you may be a superlative Christian, but you're simply not Catholic.

What's more, it is also clear that Jesus chose the Twelve to function in a different way from the other disciples, and just as clear that, when the Church began to expand in numbers around the Mediterranean, the earliest churches appointed deacons and deaconesses to help with baptisms (naked, by immersion), collecting and distributing food and funds to the needy, conducting services when no apostle was present. That hierarchical structure has continued and is not likely to change significantly. Perhaps it is imperfect, but—more or less—it nonetheless works.

Laity

Despite the fact that by far the majority of the Church are laypeople, they are defined only in negative terms: those who are not clerics and not vowed religious, which gives rise to the wrongful belief that the laity are somehow traveling second-class, if not steerage. But when the rich young man came to Jesus and asked what he must do to achieve righteousness, Jesus told him to keep the commandments. And when the man said he had done that since his earliest years, "Jesus looked straight at him with love" (Mark 10:21). That was enough. But when the young man persisted, Jesus invited him to sell all he had and come along with him, offering him the chance to be an apostle. But when the young man was unable to do that, Jesus didn't stop loving him. If it hadn't been for laypeople with some kind of money, Jesus never would have had anything to eat or a place to sleep or a cave to be buried in. The Good Samaritan was more than a source of kind words to the man in the ditch because he had a bit of money. Not to mention that this outcast layman did what the priest and levite had refused to do. (That's straight from Jesus.)

Pope Leo the Great wrote: "The sign of the cross makes kings of all those reborn in Christ and the anointing of the Holy Spirit consecrates them as priests" (*Sermo* 4:1). There are needs for sacramental and ministerial service where a priest or bishop or even the pope is neither welcome nor helpful: the family room, at the office coffee urn, the bowling alley, the locker room, the beauty shop, the boardroom, the corner bar.

Nor is it a loyal stance on the part of any Catholic to maintain "my Church, right or wrong." Just as with one's citizenship, if something is wrong, one has a duty to seek and speak the truth. If we maintain the military analogy to the hierarchical Church (or any other corporate endeavor), it is a cliché that those on the front line often know more clearly what really needs to be done and the best means to accomplish it, no matter what any others' rank or station or directives from the front office. The new *Code of Canon Law* says as much: "In accordance with the knowledge, competence, and pre-eminence which they possess, [laypeople] have the right and even at times a duty to manifest to the pastors their opinion on matters which pertain to the good of the Church, and they have a right to make their opinion known to the other Christian faithful" (CIC, can. 212 #3). "Where will we find more priests?" We already have them. They just haven't realized it yet.

How can laypeople sanctify? One could not do better than list what catechisms for generations have called the spiritual and corporal works of mercy.

The Spiritual Works of Mercy	The Corporal Works of Mercy
to admonish the sinner	to feed the hungry
to instruct the ignorant	to give drink to the thirsty
to counsel the doubtful	to clothe the naked
to comfort the sorrowful	to visit the imprisoned
to bear wrongs patiently	to shelter the homeless
to forgive all injuries	to visit the sick
to pray for the living and dead	to bury the dead

Not a bad recipe for sanctity there. Any layperson can forgive as well as any priest, perhaps not sacramentally, but just as effectively.

There are (at least) three ways in which Catholics are called to serve. One is an ecclesial inhouse way (hierarchy, clergy, eucharistic ministers, lectors, parish councils, etc.). Another is in an ecclesially sponsored way (Catholic schoolteachers, church soup kitchens, hospitals, halfway houses, etc.) Relatively few of us work in such overtly Catholic apostolates, but every Catholic is ordained an apostle—though only a handful know it or feel a need to exercise it. This third way of serving the Good News is precisely *as* a Christian working in a secular situation completely outside the Church's control, where a black shirt and white collar tab would be a drawback.

Almost every parish has an amazing array of talents: bankers, attorneys, construction people, heating experts, carpenters, architects, decorators. What if the parish were to buy one house in a rundown neighborhood and put all the skills in the parish to work on it, preparing it for a family who could never afford it? Even the teenagers and little kids could wield a paintbrush. What a unitive experience it would be. What a marshaling of diverse powers. What a service. What a clear demonstration of who we are and what we are for. What a time of grace.

The Consecrated Life

Since the beginning, Christian men and women have withdrawn almost totally from the world, some to avoid its allurements, some to devote themselves solely to the only One of truly ultimate importance. Some lived alone as hermits, others gathered into communities segregated entirely from the world in silence and regular prayer, still others opened their doors to serve the nearby community. Without them, the literature of the Western world would probably have perished forever. Far more women and men moved directly out into the world but still remained rooted in their religious traditions: "contemplatives in action."

What unites them in their diverse ways of service are the vows of poverty, celibacy, and obedience. Although their motivation seems nearly incomprehensible even to good Catholics today, especially the young, surrender of oneself to God has been an admirable, perhaps even enviable, calling through the entire history of the Church. The purpose of the vows is to liberate the individual to serve even more fully than most Catholics are called by their baptism to do. Poverty provides a kind of Christian communism in which each individual turns over all his or her earnings and receives whatever they genuinely need, as many did in the earliest churches, freeing the person from the empty promises of materialism, from worry about bills and taxes and mortgages, giving them more time and more focus on the spiritual and temporal needs of others. Celibacy frees from the legitimate demands for time and energy and concern placed on anyone who chooses to take responsibility as a spouse and parent. Obedience sets one free to be used, in consultation with a superior, in the fullest way possible, even in areas the individual might never have contemplated before. Again, no religious would ever claim the ideal is always realized, but it has been a worthy ideal and may yet be again.

The Marks of the Church

Another way to grope around the "elephant" of the Church is considering the four characteristics she has always set as ideals to embody, however imperfectly. They are captured in the Nicene Creed said at Mass: "We believe in one, holy, catholic, and apostolic Church."

(Imperfectly) One. Despite its myriad diversities, the Church is bonded, because her soul is the Holy Spirit which permeates her even into the seemingly most insignificant parts. The mop-wringer in the Empire State Building serves as truthfully and proportionately as a cardinal. Just as in marriage, the excesses of one side balance the excesses of the other: the Big Bad Beautiful Balancing Rock. No matter how we might differ on particular doctrines or disciplines, we all accept the nonnegotiables—and the primacy of Peter. However, this oneness is not assured. Even Jesus himself had to *pray* "that they may be one."

What of non-Catholic Christians? The *Catechism* clarifies that. "All who have been justified by faith in Baptism are incorporated into Christ [i.e., the Church]; they therefore have a right to be called Christians, and with good reason are accepted as brothers [and sisters] in the Lord by the children of the Catholic Church" (818).

(Imperfectly) Holy. Many very smart high school students who fancy themselves atheists plunge gleefully into research when they discover the hedonism of the renaissance popes, the atrocities of the Crusades and the Inquisition, the intransigence of the papacy against Galileo and Modernism. It's one more case of "a little knowledge" and a very narrow perspective. Anyone who tries to whitewash the Church's imperfections needs a very large bucket. But the mistakes of the few at various times, no matter how heinous and utterly contrary to the wishes of the Founder, don't negate the goodness of the many—any more than a president suborning perjury or engaging in degrading sexual dalliances negates the history of America or the ideals of its architects.

Again, the fault lies in defining "holiness" negatively, as in "flawless, morally unsullied" rather than "whole, consecrated, suffused with the otherworldly." Saint Paul repeatedly addressed his letters to "the saints," despite the fact that the body of the letter was often criticism of faults. The basic truth is not that we have *achieved* holiness but have *accepted* it being bestowed on us. This is precisely what grace means: love, undeserved. Complementarity.

(Imperfectly) Catholic. "Catholic" means all-embracing, and surely our variety is manifest: African liturgies with drums, mariachi Masses with trumpets, Chinese worship services with gongs, charismatic Masses with shouting, quiet Masses with no speaking or singing at all. We still have work to do, perhaps, in making a time of worship a welcoming experience for those who want more dramatic change, and soon, as well as those who want

no change at all. We still have to forgive one another our differences, just as every good family must. The solution is to shop around and find a way of celebrating and communicating that you and those with you feel comfortable with.

We embrace (imperfectly) those of non-Christian faith. Unlike the old Good Friday liturgies which excoriated the "perfidious Jews," those same services now speak of them as "the first to hear the word of God." As for Muslims: "The plan of salvation also includes those who acknowledge the Creator, in the first place amongst whom are the Muslims; these profess the faith of Abraham, and together with us they adore the one, merciful God, mankind's judge on the last day" (*Lumen Gentium*, 16). The operative word is "together."

(Imperfectly) Apostolic. The word applies in several senses. First, that the present Church is rooted, along the "unbroken" line of popes back to Peter and the original Twelve. Second, that as far as humanly possible, any new understandings of original doctrine and any extrapolations of doctrine to apply to cases nonexistent in apostolic times substantially agree with the original deposit of faith left by the eyewitnesses. To put it perhaps too simply, if Peter came back today and were apprised of a new situation he would say, "Yes, that's more or less what we intended." (Remember, however, that Peter, the first pope, did change his mind on at least two elements he had once thought constitutive of Christianity: the Jewish dietary laws and circumcision.) Thirdly, that the present Church is literally apostolic, *apostolos*, "one who is sent out," not only to the foreign missions but to the highways and hedges around our own homes and workplaces.

As Catholics we are and must act as emissaries. Another incontestable element of Jesus' intentions for the Church was that it not remain sequestered in the Upper Room. He sent out seventy-two disciples (not just the Twelve) on a mission, two-by-two. "As the Father sent me, so I send you" (John 20:21). Nothing could be clearer than that.

A production of *West Side Story* with overaged leads and second-rate dancers is a pretty disappointing experience. But that doesn't mean *West Side Story* isn't a deeply moving play. The original production is the ideal; every other attempt to recreate that ideal ranges from superb to mediocre to wretched. Applying that insight to weekly Masses, it's quite possible all those very intelligent people who continue to worship as Catholics have grasped a truth *beneath* the surface performance. They have made a personal "connection" to the Person the worship celebrates that is more important than the external performance.

Questions to Ponder and Discuss

✴ "The Church is essentially both human and divine, visible but endowed with invisible realities, zealous in action and dedicated to contemplation, present in the world but as a pilgrim, so constituted that in her the human is directed toward and subordinated to the divine, the visible to the invisible, action to contemplation, and this present world to that city yet to come, the object of our quest" (*Sacrosanctum Concilium*, 2). Are you comfortable with all those paradoxes?

✴ Many parents, from the best of intentions, try to project an image of perfection in the hope that it will give their children a sense of security, forgetting that, like the one in Ezekiel, all idols have clay feet. Every hero has an Achilles' heel. Similarly, when the school's brochure or the company's prospectus comes out every year, people gather at the watercooler and point to passages and snigger, "Wouldn't it be great if that were *true?*" These aren't disloyal people. In fact, most often they are very dedicated and hardworking. They are just honest enough to see the differences between the realities and the rhapsodic claims of the brochure and feel "at home" enough in the institution to ride with its flaws. Just so, some churchfolk try to project an image of the Church as (at least now) flawless and incapable of error. A kind of "creeping infallibility." Are you personally comfortable with a Catholic Church which, on the whole, is just trying to do its best with what it has at the moment? If not, it might be wise to look somewhere else for a myth that gives meaning and purpose to your life. Perhaps another galaxy?

❧ Even unconsciously restricting "the Church" to the official Church, the Vatican, can have very negative effects on the Church's possible effectiveness as an apostolic enterprise. One is "Oh, leave it to 'them.' It's their job, not mine." Another is the shepherd-sheep analogy; our purpose is to be docile (and generous). But perhaps the most telling is the suppression of so much talent and energy. No one expects any good Catholic to get up on a soapbox, but most, I suspect, are wary of being labeled "pious and pushy," leaving the apostolate to the priests and religious who signed up for that kind of thing. But brainstorm ways in which you could perhaps "infiltrate" the unquestioned certitudes of the people you deal with every week. For instance, "I read this terrific article and I photocopied it; I thought you'd enjoy it." Or merely leave the magazine lying around the office as if you'd mislaid it. "Have you ever read *The Power and the Glory?* I read it years ago, but I forgot how good it is. Want to borrow it?"

❧ When I was a boy during World War II, I was fascinated by novels about the OSS and the underground movements in France, trying to "pass" as a native and at the same time subvert the enemy's plans. Later, I spent seven years, off and on, researching the German Catholic underground during the Nazi era and the twenty-seven hundred priests who were interned in

178 WILLIAM J. O'MALLEY

the Dachau concentration camp alone. It took me a long time to realize the source of my fixation: That's what I was born to be! A subversive. That's what I do in every class: try to challenge the unexamined convictions of students, adolescent and adult, to make them at least suspect they may have settled for less out of life than they're capable of, to lure them to suspect their self-protectiveness might inhibit them, and then perhaps even to seduce them to consider Christianity. As you know well, conversion is a very, very slow process. Reflect on your own unique journey to this point in your understanding of the Church. Could you use what you've learned to intrigue someone else?

❧ Scripture: Acts 2:1-10; I Peter 2:9-10; Ephesians 4:1-6; I Corinthians 12:25-31; Hebrews 13:14

❧ *Catechism:* 777-780, 802-810, 866-870, 934-945, 960-962

You must learn to understand the "Ah!" of things!
—An anonymous Zen master

⁕ 13 ⁕

THE SACRAMENTS

Most Catholic symbols sacred to me as a boy seem drained of any effectiveness today. I don't know many who wear a Miraculous Medal or a scapular or carry rosaries. And yet, because we're human, we do invest a "sacredness" in physical objects which somehow embody a reality which is itself nonphysical: a wedding ring, a varsity letter, a yellow ribbon. That lone student motionless in front of behemoth tanks in Tiananmen Square says more of gallantry in helplessness than any treatise. Games begin with "The Star Spangled Banner," and even if that hymn carries no sacredness most times, God help any corpulent comedian who mocks it. July Fourth would be just a day, without fireworks. The Olympics have to begin with the torch. Because it's *special*—in a world where "special" doesn't have much meaning anymore.

However, if that need for symbols is true, it is difficult to make the quiet, homely symbols of the sacraments meaningful in a world where "Ah!" is rare, held back except for a spectacular dive on "Wide World of Sports," a new Trans Am, a great body.

A wise old borscht-circuit comedian once said to me, "Father, we've forgotten the taste of bread." He's right. Bread is so ready-to-hand for most of us that we hardly notice it, except as a vehicle for something else like ham and cheese or peanut butter and jelly. It no longer comes fresh and crusty from the oven, tanging your nostrils and making your mouth water. It comes wrapped in deathless plastic, presliced, with all the taste of putty, guaranteed not to offend or gratify anyone. Like so much else in our lives: taken for granted, homogenized, dull.

In fact, all the elements of all the sacraments are like the salt in the Gospel: they've lost their savor, not because they've literally gone flat in themselves, but they've become devalued simply because we have such an excess of them. Wine is really meaningless now, unless you have too much of it. Water doesn't mean for us what it meant in the hills of Galilee or the wilderness at Jericho—where water was a matter of life or death. We've got swimming pools full of it; we can stand under the shower for fifteen or twenty minutes. Oil used to symbolize empowerment, anointing kings and knights; the very name "Messiah" means "the Anointed One." Now oil is for suntans, salads, and french fries. What were once the staples of simpler lives have now become commonplace, pedestrian, stale, flat. "Tomorrow and tomorrow and tomorrow creeps in this petty pace from day to day."

Is that all there is?

Each of the sacraments is a rite of conversion: a call to a larger life than we had settled for. Most often, the sacrament's "gifts" are not palpable infusions of vitality and grace, but rather the paradoxical gift and grace of *challenge*. Baptism invites us beyond the security of our own families out into the opportunity and assurance of the Family of God. Confirmation affirms that call in a stronger way, usually at least somewhere near the time of life when one is prepared by adolescence for greater challenges. The Eucharist challenges us to embody Jesus and his mission, to break ourselves up and hand round the pieces. Reconciliation challenges us to shuck off the comfortable bad habits and come alive again. The anointing of the sick challenges the sufferer to see this ambush as a call, at least for the moment, to offer ourselves to others for their kindness, to face this unwelcome intrusion as Jesus faced his passion and death. No question that marriage and holy orders are challenges, to leave behind the autonomous life and serve.

There is also a kind of "no matter what" about each of the sacraments. Baptism "says" that no matter what you do, you will always be welcome home here when you choose to come. Confirmation says, quite simply, "We need you, no matter what you think of your shortcomings." Eucharist says, "No matter what you *feel*, you are never truly alone." Reconciliation says that no sin is beyond the forgiveness of Jesus Christ; no matter what you have done, no matter how repellent you think it is, it is not repellent to us, as long as you are willing to come home and share it with us. The anointing of the sick says that, no matter what you've done in your life, we are your family and another family awaits you beyond death. Marriage and holy orders say I will stick with you, with this vocation, with the challenge, till I die.

Since the sacraments follow and give shape to the Christian life, from birth to death, they are often handled sequentially in order of their reception or, as the *Catechism*, logically, beginning with the sacraments of initiation (as they were in the early Church when most entered as adults—baptism, confirmation, Eucharist), then sacraments of healing (reconciliation, the anointing of the sick), and, finally, sacraments of vocation (marriage and holy orders). I would like rather to treat them psychologically, beginning with the ones easiest for a beginner to understand, the moments in life that simply cry out for "something special" even for those who have no religious affiliation or have left it long behind: marriage, birth, and death. Then an order based on what I suspect would be the order of interest for those engaged with this book: Eucharist, reconciliation, confirmation, and, finally, holy orders.

We begin with the easiest sacraments to understand. Three moments in life cry out for religious symbol and ritual, when people who "don't need church" *do* need church, moments with too much "Ah!" in them for any context other than a religious one: marriage, birth, and death. When two people vow unconditional responsibility for one another till death, it just doesn't "happen" in a J.P.'s office. When an infant is born, even if the parents don't practice, the child *has* to be baptized, not out of fear of hell but "because it's so *important!*" And at the moment of a loved one's death, God is no longer escapable.

Matrimony (*Catechism,* 1601-1666; Genesis 1:26-28; Colossians 3:12-17; John 2:1-11). Marriage is the easiest sacrament to understand as a sacrament, an outward sign of a genuine inner change, a change that's actually *felt* not only by the bridal couple but by those in attendance at the wedding. A wedding—even outside a religious context—is very clearly a change, a rite of passage from independence to partnership. A marriage is the basic human experience of what creative, salvific, redemptive love means: you are not alone, you are not meaningless, you and I, together, are "at home."

In *The Skin of Our Teeth,* Maggie Antrobus, whose husband is going off with a floozie, says: "I didn't marry you because you were perfect, George. I didn't even marry you because I loved you. I married you because you gave me a promise. That promise made up for your faults. And the promise I gave you made up for mine. Two imperfect people got married, and it was that promise that made the marriage. . . . And when our children were growing up, it wasn't a house that protected them; and it wasn't our love that protected them—it was that promise."

A marriage is not a contract signed in an office; it is a commitment in the heart—surely not in the analytical mind!—to take responsibility for another person "all the days of my life." You can't "try out" a permanent promise. Contracts deal with things; covenants deal with people. Both the Hebrew and the Christian Scriptures expressed the relationship between God and us with language taken from an understanding of an ideal marriage. In turn, we can understand an ideal marriage by understanding God's love for us: I am with you, "no matter what."

The wedding is only one climactic moment in a long process of *becoming* married. Every married couple is *a lot* more married today than on the day they first vowed responsibility for one another. That process began when the couple began dating, getting gradually to know one another, easy with one another, friendly, testing to find out if this person just might be Mister or Miss Right. When the relationship begins to become exclusive, the couple reaches another stage into a deeper commitment to one another, which can be very precarious when the feelings are overpowering and the commitment is not—because of schooling, finances, unreadiness to take lifelong responsibility—even full responsibility for his or her *self*. Till then, no one is ready.

When the two finally make a resolve to become engaged and make public their intention to commit to one another, the commitment deepens further, and as in all love relationships the more one invests in the other, the more painful betrayal can be. That doesn't mean that betrayal, that a "little death," cannot be turned into a rebirth. If the couple can get through those trials—and still love one another—the "little death" has only made the love stronger. Scar tissue is toughest.

The two Testaments begin with the creation and union of a

man and woman and end with the wedding feast of the Lamb. The vocation to marriage is written in the very nature of man and woman. "Therefore a man leaves his father and mother and cleaves to his wife, and they become one flesh" (Genesis 2:24). Jesus performed his first miracle at the wedding feast of Cana and often compared his Kingdom to a wedding feast. Saint Paul wrote, "Husbands, love your wives, as Christ loved the Church and gave himself up for her, that he might sanctify her" (Ephesians 5:25).

In the Western Catholic Church, the *couple* confer the sacrament on one another, and the clerical minister is merely the Church's witness. The essential element of the sacrament is not the specific words spoken but the assent within each of their minds and hearts to take responsibility for the other person till one of them dies. The man and woman would be married if they, with all sincerity, pledged themselves to one another as Tony and Maria do in *West Side Story,* but the union is both challenged and strengthened and insured a greater chance of survival when the vows are pledged, knowingly and fearlessly and responsibly before and to the Church.

Such a marriage is a covenant guaranteed by God's fidelity, witnessed to by the Church with a promise of her unfailing support—but that does not assure "happily ever after" is in the bag. Like every other sacrament, marriage is a gift of challenge, and just as it takes effort, creativity, and dedication to remain faithful to one's baptism and confirmation, it takes those same qualities—and many more—to remain faithful to one's marriage, most important among them the gift to one another of total self-disclosure and the gift of forgiveness.

Marriage aims at a total personal unity—and *yet* with each partner maintaining a unique self, not absorbed into the other, keeping a self who is still intrigued and intriguing. It is a total self-giving, and *yet* with a self still capable of saying, "I think you're wrong." It is undivided and exclusive, and *yet* capable of including other genuine friends, of both sexes, and of course children who will force their way into what had been an exclusive relationship. If you are not comfortable with paradox, it's wise not to become married. In fact, it's wise not to consider Christianity!

Marriage between a Catholic and a non-Catholic Christian (a mixed marriage) or between a Catholic and a non-baptized person (disparity of cult) need not constitute an insurmountable obstacle to a successful marriage. But they do call for prudence when each one's way of connecting to God is important to both parties. It can become a source of serious tension: How do we handle the religious education of the children? Will they ask for confirmation or bar mitzvah? Where will we worship, separately or together? Whose holidays do we celebrate? (And in these questions it is of absolute importance that the decision be the *couples'*, not their parents' decision.) Often, the sad solution is to let all religious practice slip into mere indifference because it lessens the squabbles. In order for the marriage to be valid in the Catholic Church, the couple must obtain an express permission (a dispensation), which is usually readily given but does act as an opportunity to make the couple consider a source of difficulties they may not have considered in the flush of romance.

In recent years, a different source of abrasion has arisen regarding marriage when the Catholic party or parties have not practiced any religion at all, and it seems to the minister whom they ask to receive their vows that religion is less than even peripheral in their lives. They don't worship or pray. It becomes clear even to the most openhearted cleric that the only reason they ask for a Catholic wedding is to placate the parents or as an excuse for all the nonessentials that have become so madly dominant in weddings now: the *Trumpet Voluntary,* the brides-maids' gowns, the flowers, and especially the reception. At such times, some priests ask the two about to marry to sit down and

186 WILLIAM J. O'MALLEY

write out why they want a priest or a deacon to officiate, not just as an old friend but *as* a representative of the Roman Catholic Church. The results are often eye-opening for them. If not, I for one would find problems of conscience offering them the blessing of a community that really means nothing to them.

Marriage is the stable basis for the future of humankind, the cradle of children, the nest of their nurturance, the primary source of their learning. The family which springs from marriage is the most fundamental "at home" there is, for all its members, for all their lives.

Baptism (1213-1284; Matthew 2:13-17; John 20:19-33; Romans 6:3-5). *Baptizein* means to "plunge" or "immerse" because in that form it is symbolic of being plunged into Christ's death and emerging, gasping, into new life in a new family beyond the birth family: the People of God, the Body of Christ.

Genesis shows Yahweh's Spirit brooding over the primeval waters from which all life came, the waters of Noah's Flood dawned into a new beginning, and above all the crossing of the Red Sea was an embodiment of freedom and the crossing of the Jordan into Canaan an image of a brand new life. Baptism was also Jesus' entrance from an ordinary, pedestrian life into a life of service and sacrifice for others, and he referred to his coming Passion as a "baptism with which I must be baptized" (Mark 10:38), his life-giving death.

In the earliest years, when adult baptism was the norm, the candidate prepared heart and mind with someone more knowledgeable, then after a series of introductory rituals received all three of the rites of initiation at night, usually Holy Saturday. He or she was immersed in water by a deacon or deaconess, then led into the house where the community had gathered to have the bishop confirm the baptism and then to join all the assembled for the first time in the Eucharist. Vatican II reinstated that order for adults in the Rite of Christian Initiation of Adults.

The symbols—like all metaphors—need to be "decompacted." The sign of the cross, from the officiant and all Christians present, is the very first welcoming ritual, symbolically imprinting *the* symbol which distills everything Christianity means: rebirth through death. After the celebrant offers a segment of the gospel and a brief homily, he leads those present in a series of petitions for those to be welcomed into the community and prayers rejecting evil, in preparation for the first anointing with the oil of catechumens empowering them to confess the faith—which adult candidates do for themselves, and which infants profess through their parents and godparents. Then begins the essential rite. Three times the celebrant pours water over the candidates' heads, saying, "[Name], I baptize you in the name of the Father and of the Son and of the Holy Spirit." Then the second anointing with chrism, blessed by the bishop each Holy Thursday, the same oil with which priests are consecrated, incorporating the baptized into the Body of Christ as priest, prophet, and peers of the Realm. The baptized receive a white garment as a symbol of "putting on Christ" and are given a candle lit from the Easter candle signifying their mission to become the light of the world. The rite concludes with the Lord's Prayer and a final blessing.

As Saint Paul writes, "When anyone is joined to Christ, he or she is a new being; the old is gone, the new is come" (2 Corinthians 5:17). "You know that your bodies are now parts of the body of Christ" (1 Corinthians 6:15). No sin whatever can erase that union.

I confess (again) to one more hesitation in the usual catechesis: the emphasis on the relation of sin and baptism. In the case of adult converts to be baptized, I have no such hesitation. Anyone who has reached adolescence is capable of reason and therefore of a sense of sin. Nor do I have any hesitation of admitting that even a child is capable of moral evil. As we saw, moral evil (culpable or not) is a violation of the objective

188 WILLIAM J. O'MALLEY

"horizontal" web of relationships we have with everyone and everything on this planet. Sin, however, adds a different, "vertical" dimension to that same act; it also ruptures a relationship with God. Until an individual is capable of understanding that relationship and personally accepting it, she or he is capable of moral evil but not capable of rending and insulting a relationship they're in no way aware of. When children are old enough to understand that some actions are wrong *in themselves* (not just because others "arbitrarily" claim they are) and capable of some initial sense of God's existence, presence, and generosity, then I believe they have become capable of sin. But I have a very difficult time associating evil with *infant* baptism.

When I look at an infant, making sucky-kissy noises, a being who can't control its own bowels yet, I can't accept that it is responsible for *anything*, nor can I love a "God" who would reprehend such an innocent as guilty of a "debt." Sin is about death; baptism is about life. Baptism is public acknowledgment that this child has been invited into the Trinity Family, and this moment physicalizes that belief for the child's parents: This child will never die. There is no doubt that this child is—by the mere fact of its animal aspect—*prone* to sin, what the catechisms always call "concupiscence," a longing for the corruptive. But this infant is not yet "tainted" or "stained." What baptism says about sin, I believe, is that when this child sins—and she inevitably will—there will never be a time when she will not be welcomed home. No matter what.

Anointing the Sick (1499-1532; James 5:14-15; Luke 4:38-40; Mark 16:17-18). Sickness does not attack just the body. It attacks a total human being. The illness—whether acute, chronic, or terminal—forces a person to confront the limitations that bodiliness imposes on our souls: our hopes, our dreams, our desire to be meaningful.

All sacraments are about death and resurrection; that's what the Gospel is about. Every philosopher, from Buddha to Karl Marx, begins with suffering: Why are we the only species which knows things are not as they "ought" to be? Viktor Frankl, a psychiatrist who survived the death camps, says that, even for a prisoner who did nothing to deserve condemnation, the individual was left with the ultimate human freedom: the choice of one's *attitude* toward this unmerited suffering. If there was no God, of course, there would be simply no reason for this anguish, no purpose, no meaning. "That's . . . just the way things are." But if one believes in God, there simply *must* be a purpose to all this. Admittedly, we can't know what that purpose is; but there must *be* one. The anointing of the sick will very rarely heal the anguish of the body. It is intended to heal the anguish of the soul. It is one more rite of conversion—of attitude.

Anyone who has suffered in or served in a hospital or nursing home knows the spectrum of attitudes in response to undeserved suffering. Some patients rail and rant "against the dying of the light." Others withdraw into almost autistic solitude and self-absorption. But some few startle those around them with an incandescent acceptance. I knew a merchant seaman named Bill Fold who was in a terminal-cancer ward. He had a laryngectomy and could communicate only on paper. He also had tuberculosis and so was in isolation. I said to him one day, "Bill, it must get very lonely." And he wrote on his pad, "Yes, but isn't it wonderful God trusts me enough to give it to me!" No need for canonization there. I asked if there were anything I could do for him, and he wrote he'd truly love to be anointed. At that time, "Extreme Unction" was reserved to those in imminent danger of death, and doctors said Bill could last for months. But I threw caution and laws to the wind and gave him the full anointing. When we finished, tears puddling in his eyes, Bill wrote, "I'm so grateful. Is there anything I could do for you?" And I said, "Bill, when you get there, mention my name, okay?" And he wrote, "I shall." And that night he died.

As Isaiah said of the Messiah, "He himself took our sickness and carried away our diseases" (Matthew 8:17; Isaiah 53:4). Jesus asked us for faith: "Don't be afraid, only believe" (Mark 5:36). As the crucifixion demonstrates, suffering is the road to transcendence. Just as guilt has value only when we turn it into responsibility, suffering becomes meaningful only when it opens our minds and hearts to wider horizons. Sister Thea Bowman, dying of cancer, wrote: "Perhaps it's an incentive for struggling human beings to reach out to one another, to help one another, to love one another, to be blessed and strengthened and humanized in the process."

"In my name . . . they will place their hands on sick people, and they will get well." Sometimes, in fact, those anointed do get well. Just as doctors say a patient's negative attitude can cause psychosomatic diseases, so too they believe a positive attitude helps them get well. But this sacrament, even though based on Jesus' own miracles, isn't some kind of magic. Its deepest purpose is healing the soul, making peace with the things that—at least for now—can't be changed. It sanctifies, makes holy (whole), incorporates this unwelcome challenge into the patient's life so he or she can find peace with it. It means to serve the same purpose for those losing a loved one. Anointing the sick is not so much a cure as a sign of *conversion*.

The *Catechism* puts the order of the service succinctly: "Like all the sacraments the anointing of the sick is a liturgical and communal celebration, whether it takes place in the family home, a hospital, or church, for a single sick person or a whole group of sick persons. It is very fitting to celebrate it within the Eucharist, the memorial of the Lord's Passover" (1517).

Funerals. Although they are not a sacrament separate from the Mass, the ritual of a wake and funeral can also be the occasion for a sacramental conversion in the community, opening up horizons made commonplace by habit. It is a formal opportunity for the family and loved ones to yield to an essential internal action: letting go, acknowledging that life must go on without the person who has died. It is also a provocation to contemplate the limits which death places on human life. Acknowledging this present loss makes the other people one can still enjoy all the more cherished. And it is salutary for ourselves. Without a felt sense of death, we live a life deceiving ourselves that we have an endless number of days, not valuing each day as precious because it is precarious.

The funeral itself is a true microcosm of what the Church means. Just as the person was welcomed at the church door as an infant, the priest welcomes the deceased and his or her family, blesses the coffin with water and covers it with a white cloth as at baptism. The procession passes up the main aisle, and the coffin is placed under the Easter candle, a symbol of resurrection and burning life. At the offertory, the priest or deacon incenses the coffin, the smoke symbolizing our prayers for the deceased. After communion, when some family member or friend has given a personal eulogy, the priest in the name of the whole assembly and the whole Church commends the deceased on his or her final journey. At the grave, the minister prays with and for those gathered around it, asking for comfort, consolation, strength, trust in God for them and for eternal rest for the dead. Then he says— to both the living and the dead—"Go in the peace of Christ."

Eucharist (1322-1419; Matthew 26:26-30; 18:20; Luke 24:13-35). The Eucharist is the core of the Christian life. It is the *Most* Blessed Sacrament. In fact, all ministries and apostolates are rooted in it. It is, quite literally, the source of our *communion* with Christ and one another. Our faith is founded in it and fed by it. It embodies the death and resurrection not only of Christ but of each of us as well. Sin and death have no place in the Mass, except to be rejected. It is an image of all the parables Jesus told about the Kingdom of God, here and hereafter, as a wedding feast in which we are conjoined to him in a new covenant of loving. Just as the two disciples on the road to Emmaus, we recognize Jesus "in the breaking of the bread." The very word "Eucharist" means thanksgiving. For everything.

In the time of Jesus, bread and wine were the staples of life. Moreover, in the Hebrew Scriptures bread and wine were offered to Yahweh in celebration of the harvest, just as Americans celebrate Thanksgiving. In the Passover meal, they remind Jews of the haste in which they had to prepare for their liberation.

It is quite clear not only that the Last Supper was a climactic moment in the life of the new Christian community but that it was the focus of unity for the earliest churches and that it has continued so down through the ages, among the Eastern Orthodox and Western Catholics and all the various forms of Protestantism (no matter how they differ regarding its essence).

First of all, the Eucharist is an act of *thanksgiving*—for everything. When people ask me, "How ya doin'?" I answer with irritating regularity, "Probably better than I deserve." They usually remonstrate and say of course I deserve. . . . What? I didn't deserve to be born. After that, everything's gravy. If you think of all the people you love, all things and activities that give you joy, and if you then realize that—without that initial gift of existence—you'd never have even known any of them, wow! Granted, if you'd never existed you'd never know what you'd missed, but you do exist and, again, wow! But when you take everything for granted, as if you'd somehow merited it all, then it's difficult to be grateful or give thanks.

The commandments enjoin us to "Keep holy the Sabbath day," and there is a law of the Church which enjoins us to worship every week. As we saw before, rules and laws are written for people too self-centered or lazy or busy to think for themselves. Just as there really ought to be no need for a law forbidding the abuse of one's own children, there surely ought to be no need to force anyone honorable to give thanks, often, for . . . everything.

The Eucharist is also a *memorial*, in which we remember and celebrate our profound belief that, by the death and resurrection of Jesus we celebrate at each Mass, we have been set free from the fear of death and from the fear of ultimate meaninglessness that the unbeliever must face. Like the Hebrews at Passover, we remember that we have been liberated, once for all, and we celebrate it not just once a year but every week.

And the Eucharist is a *sacrifice*. "This is my Body which will be given up *for* you. . . . this is a cup of my blood. . . . it will be shed *for* you and *for* all, so *that* sins may be forgiven." As we are incorporated into the Body of Christ, we offer ourselves through our Head, Christ, to the Father, as the entire People of God and as each individual member, not only those currently present but those all over the world and those who have gone beyond it.

Jesus' first announcement of the Eucharist divided the disciples. When Jesus said, "Whoever eats my flesh and drinks my blood has eternal life" (John 6:54), many left him. When he asked the rest if they would go, too, Peter answered for me: "Lord, to whom would we go?"

Perhaps the single most important reason I am a Catholic, rather than some other kind of Christian, is my unshakable belief in transubstantiation, that—somehow—the bread and wine truly *become* the Body and Blood of Christ. I can give no rational, left-brain proof for this belief, other than my conviction that the God who could make a universe out of nothing can do anything. Nor can I explain *how* such a transformation can occur, any more than I can explain how the universe came from nothing. I can no more explain it than I can explain why I have remained a Jesuit for fifty years or that my friends can explain why they married one another and stayed together through thick and thin. I just know, implacably, that it is *right*.

The Protestant theologian, Karl Barth, articulates what a difference it makes to believe that the presence of the risen Lord actually exists not only in the assembly and in God's Word and in the priest but actually *in* the bread and wine:

At those times when the task of being ministers of the divine word, as we of the Reformed Churches say, has oppressed us, have we not all felt a yearning for the rich services of Catholicism, and for the enviable role of the priest at the altar? When he elevates the *Sanctissimum*, with its full measure of that meaning and power which the *material* symbol enjoys over the symbol of the human word, the double grace of the sacrificial death and the incarnation of the Son of God is not only preached in words but actually takes place in his hands.

What Holy Communion *ought* to do within our souls is first of all to focus ourselves, at least for that short while, on what is truly important in our lives—that we are eternal, here and now, that we are enlivened in our innermost selves by the Energy which is the source of all existence. As food nourishes our bodies, and learning nourishes our minds, so this act of ingesting Christ should nourish and empower our souls. It commits us to the same mission Jesus so clearly and consistently fulfilled: all the spiritual and corporal works of mercy.

The Eucharist is the manna that sustains us on our journey through the plastic wilderness.

Reconciliation (1422-1498; Luke 23:32-43; Acts 10:42-44; Colossians 1:13-15). Whenever Jesus performed a miracle of healing, it was most often in the context of forgiveness of sins, a sign of the intermingled physical and moral lives of us all. Like each one of the other sacraments, this one is also a rite of conversion, from a smaller life to a larger one.

Reconciliation is the most obvious challenge to *convertere*, "to do a complete turnabout." We realize that for too long we have drifted along a road of slovenly habits, half-measures, self-deceptions, and that the only honorable thing to do is resolve to go back to the first wrong turn and start over again fresh. Like the prodigal son, we pull ourselves up short and say, "Wait a minute. What am I doing here?" We no longer feel "at home," either within the groups among whom we live and work or, more importantly, inside our own selves. So in that moment of clarity and honesty, we pick ourselves up and head for "home."

Going to confession is no more pleasant than lifting weights, but those who lift weights find merit in it, either athletic or cosmetic, and so they dedicate themselves to it. A visit to the dentist or doctor isn't pleasant either, but those of us who have our wits about us realize it's essential if we're going to catch any defects before they get beyond repair. You could say pretty much the same about the sacrament of reconciliation.

Perhaps the *most* basic virtue is honesty, honesty with things and people as they are, but even more fundamentally, honesty with *oneself*—without self-delusive excuses, without defensive euphemisms, without holding back. Kid everybody else, but for God's sake (literally) don't ever kid yourself for very long. Confession is the sacrament of complete honesty.

The same old self-serving objection arises about confession as about public worship: "Why can't I just go out into the woods?" Just as with worship, such a humble submission to God by oneself is praiseworthy, but again the first question is: "When was the last time you *did* it?" Merely on the human level, there is something clean and clear about having to find the words to tell another sinful human being the ways in which you have definitely fallen short of your call as a human being and an adopted child of the Trinity Family. It's embarrassing, but it's forthright and in a very real sense cauterizing. But on the supernatural level, there is no escaping that Jesus did say about worship, "Do *this* in memory of me," and to Peter, "I will give you the keys of the kingdom of heaven, and whatever you loose on earth shall be loosed in heaven" (Matthew 16:19). If the Jesus we claim freed us from the fear of death and annihilation asks it, who can refuse?

To my mind, the penance the priest offers—and whatever penance one chooses during Advent or Lent—ought to be positive, effecting something good, rather than negative, depriving the penitent of something. Creative self-assertion, rather than self-denial. Offering one of the spiritual or temporal works of mercy is a way. Whenever a mother confesses, she almost always mentions shortness of temper with the children, so her penance is, a half-hour before the school bus arrives, kick off your shoes, sit down with a cup of tea, and entertain Jesus in your home. For a hardworking mother that really *is* a penance, but no mother has ever refused it. Conversely, when a boy confesses, he almost inevitably mentions disrespect for his parents, so his penance is, when you get home from school, say, "Mom, is there any way I could help out more?"

In the gospels, when Jesus dealt one-on-one with a sinner— "the woman known as a sinner in the town," the adulterous woman, the Samaritan woman at the well, the prodigal son, the repentant Peter—he never once gave a retaliatory penance. Which brings up the question of *atonement*, one I think is often handled more from the point of view of an accountant than that of Jesus. No doubt, on a strictly *human* level, there are sins which demand remuneration: return or compensation for stolen goods, the restoration of someone's reputation, recompense for physical injuries. But—again judging by Jesus—I don't agree with those who say we also have to make some kind of atonement to a God who, by definition, can't even be ruffled, much less angered. According to Jesus, the father of the prodigal son neither asked the specifics of how the boy wasted his father's money nor demanded a full repayment—or any payment at all. To my mind, once the priest has given God's absolution, God's forgotten the sins ever happened. God holds no grudges, because Jesus held no grudges and because he forbade us to hold them. We don't need to "expiate" or "make satisfaction for" our sins, as if God were a banker and not a Father. There is no longer a rift between the sinner and God. That's been *healed*. But there surely is a rift which still needs healing: the rift within one's own soul. That's where prayer helps the sinner become once again "at home," within his or herself and within the Church.

As for purgatory, I don't think the way Jesus dealt with sinners allows for a doctrine which says there is a "temporal punishment due to sin" even *after* the sinner has sincerely begged forgiveness and God has definitively forgiven. Nor can I comprehend a kind of financial system whereby we offer prayers and penances to "buy off" certain "time" our friends and relatives have to "pay" in order to atone. Purgatory is *beyond* time. But I do think there *has* to be a purgatory, not for debtors to wipe out a debt but for those who die incapable of genuine joy. They have to learn honestly to love full-heartedly, to forgive, to surrender center stage to Someone Else. Purgatory is a state where they learn all of the things they were put *here* to learn.

Confirmation (1285-1321; Isaiah 11:2-9; Jeremiah 1:1-8; Luke 4:16-19). Confirmation is a sacrament of the Holy Spirit, the same Spirit who brooded over the waters at that beginning, who rested upon Jesus at his baptism, who descended on the disciples in storm and fire on Pentecost, whom the Apostles called down on converts. It is the Spirit who is the soul of the Mystical Body of Christ, who animates each and all of us with the life of God.

In the earliest centuries, confirmation was conferred immediately after baptism and just before first Communion, but the growth of infant baptisms, the spread of the Church over vast areas, and the expansion of dioceses made it impossible for the bishop to be on site to ratify all the baptisms. Thus, at least in the Western Church, confirmation comes quite a few years after the baptism of "cradle Christians." Although this has been the practice for most of the Church's life, purists insist that it be given as closely as possible to baptism, sometimes as early as age seven when, supposedly, the power of reason begins to emerge. Anyone actively engaged in teaching the young knows that the capacity for objective reasoning does not even begin to emerge until the later years of high school—and not in all. Others—perhaps more numerous but surely less influential—believe confirmation could become a real rite of passage after puberty, a way to help willing young people assimilate the very real new relationship with the community their newly found adult bodies invites them to. It could be a powerful declaration of Christian maturity in which the Church not only confirms the individual's baptism but also the individuals personally and freely confirm a baptism chosen for them before they could understand. But since by far the majority of the readers of this book are young adults or older, the point is relatively moot.

Again, to decompact the symbols. Wrestlers and other athletes anointed their bodies with oil as they prepared to contend in the games, and those confirmed have a new responsibility to contend with stronger forces than they had to face before. It also was a source of healing for bruises and wounds. In a connection to the Eucharist, oil is also the force that binds the elements of bread. Most important, just as in baptism and in holy orders, anointing with chrism is a sign of *consecration*. "He has put his seal on us and given us his Spirit in our hearts as a guarantee" (2 Corinthians 1:22). When Jesus predicted that new Christians would be turned over to the Jewish and pagan powers, he told them not to fear, because his Spirit was in them to speak.

At the outset of the rite, the bishop raises his hands over the candidates and prays that they may have the Spirit of wisdom, understanding, right judgment, courage, knowledge, reverence, wonder, and awe in the presence of God. Then, imposing his palm on each head, at the same time he anoints each forehead with the chrism on his thumb, saying, "Accept this sign of the gift of the Holy Spirit." Then he embraces them in the sign of peace signifying the union and concern of all those present and of the whole Church.

Holy Orders (1536-1600; Hebrews 5:5-6; 1 Timothy 3:8-13; 4:6-16). "There are different ways of serving but the same Lord" (1 Corinthians 12:5). The whole Church and all its members is a priestly people. Our task is to sanctify the world, enliven it with the Spirit of Christ. Ordination is a consecration, a "setting-apart" of individuals to serve us, the frontline apostles, empowering us through the sacraments to serve more fruitfully. Teaching, conducting divine worship, navigating the Barque of Peter. The ordained—the clergy—are not "the Church," but without them the Church would not be, just as (reverting to the military metaphor) an army is a pointless rabble without a commander, line officers, non-coms, and footsoldiers.

The pope is the successor to Peter, the rock, Vicar of Christ, that is, a person empowered to perform the functions of another, the Head of the Mystical Body. As the successors of the Twelve, bishops united with the pope are responsible for the well-being of the whole Church and in their separate dioceses for the instruction, sacramental life, and coordination of the Church in that locality. In the same way, the priests of a diocese united with the bishop care for the needs of the faithful in even smaller areas, parishes. Deacons are ordained to share in the ministry of the word, pastoral organization, and the service of charity.

In classical Latin, the word *ordo* designated certain groups in society, as the senatorial order, the order of scribes, the order of matrons—like a medieval guild. So in the Church there were orders of catechumens, penitents, deacons, priests, and bishops. And although holy orders and matrimony are primarily rites of mission, they are also rites of initiation into a whole new way of life and a whole new relationship with the Church.

There are two somewhat conflicting functions of the

ministerial priesthood. First and foremost is a spiritual power: to call the risen Christ into bread and wine, to forgive sins, to preach the word of God, to heal, to witness vows. From what we can gather about the earliest churches, that was the service they were ordained to provide the community. But as the Church grew from isolated communities into an institution stretching across the known world, in order to preserve unity there had to be a structure. Thus, over the centuries priesthood developed a second function: maintaining order, orthodoxy, and faithfulness to the Gospel. The two roles of minister ("servant") and official ("manager") conflict insofar as the first calls for empathy, vulnerability, a willingness to be used by Christ and by the people, while the other calls for assertiveness, decisiveness, directness. Everyone empowered by holy orders must struggle with that.

The *Decree on the Ministry and Life of Priests* says: "They cannot be ministers of Christ unless they are witnesses and dispensers of a life other than this earthly one. But they cannot be of service to human beings if they remain strangers to the life and conditions of human beings. Their ministry itself by a special title forbids them to be conformed to this world. Yet at the same time this ministry requires that they live in this world among human beings" (3).

I have always thought of the ministerial priest (at whichever level) as a *lens,* focusing the prayers of the faithful to God and the transforming power of God back to the people. When I preside at a wedding (a sacrament the couple confers on one another, not the priest), I stand down in the aisle. The couple submits their vows not to me but to the Church, so I ask the members of the Church assembled to signify their approval by applauding as loudly as they can. The same is true for the priest's function at all the other sacraments. He is an instrument, a stand-in for Christ, no matter what his personal worthiness or lack of it.

The *Catechism* makes a prudent concession: "This presence of Christ in the minister is not to be understood as if [the minister] were preserved from all human weaknesses, the spirit of domination, error, even sin. The power of the Holy Spirit does not guarantee all acts of ministers in the same way. While this guarantee extends to the sacraments, so that even the minister's sin cannot impede the fruit of grace, in many other acts the minister leaves human traces that are not always signs of fidelity to the Gospel and consequently can harm the apostolic fruitfulness of the Church" (1550). Again, the Church is an ideal embodied by victims of original sin. Ordination does not confer or guarantee openmindedness, openheartedness, open-handedness. What it does confer and guarantee is the effectiveness of the sacraments on a receptive candidate, "no matter what."

The American bishops, in *As One Who Serves,* compare the priest's role to an orchestra conductor: "The conductor succeeds when he or she stimulates the best performance from each player and combines their individual efforts into a pattern of sound, achieving the vision of the composer" (46). Of course, the model of all priests is Jesus' dealing with his own small, fractious group of followers. He taught them, served them, even to the point of getting down on his knees and washing their feet. He was patient with their doubts, their skepticism, their wrong-headed ideas of what is important. He even forgave their desertion. The priesthood of Jesus, then, was in response to *their* needs—both the ones they openly brought to him and the needs they didn't even realize they had.

A local bishop is chosen by the Bishop of Rome and ordained by several of his fellow bishops anointing him and laying their hands on his head as a symbol of sharing power. Similarly, priests are trained to the satisfaction of their superiors, presented to the bishop for anointing, and welcomed into the

202 WILLIAM J. O'MALLEY

priesthood by other priests laying their hands on the new priests' heads. At the ordination of deacons only the bishop imposes hands, signifying that this man is an emissary of the bishop to assist at the Eucharist, bless marriages, proclaim the Gospel and preach, preside over funerals, and offer themselves to ministries of charity such as visiting the sick and bringing them communion.

Celibacy. "Jesus answered, 'There are different reasons why men cannot marry: some, because they were born that way; others, because men made them that way; and others do not marry for the sake of the Kingdom of heaven. Let him who can accept this teaching do so'" (Matthew 19:12). It is interesting to note that immediately after that, people who had married and had children brought them to be blessed by Jesus, who never married. Right after that, the rich young man came and, even though he couldn't yield to that self-offering, Jesus still looked straight at him and loved him, even if he "only" kept the commandments.

A well-to-do Jewish agnostic once asked a priest why he was celibate, and the priest answered, "I know love isn't quantifiable, but my energy is very much quantifiable. I figure that, if I were married, my wife and kids would deserve my *best* loving. But loving three or four people that intensely isn't enough for me. So I keep my ability to love 'unfocused,' so that whoever shows up gets the full shot."

Surely a priest has more time, mobility, and freedom from legitimate entanglements in order to serve. Yet how can a celibate empathize with the problems of married people when he's never been married? In the first place, a celibate priest is still a human being, and has himself suffered what most human beings have had to suffer in relationships. He knows what it's like to struggle against selfishness—in himself as well as in others, with people who refuse to change for their own good, with being taken advantage of. And his vow of celibacy does not surrender his sexuality, only the use of it. He has wrestled with the mystery of sex quite possibly more than married people, again in himself but also with many others. And, one supposes, if marital difficulties are a large part of the problems brought to him, he has probably made more effort even than most married people to study and understand marriage. What's more, most marital problems are not problems with sex but problems between people. And the priest is a "people."

One could argue that the priest has never had the chance to share a real body-and-soul relationship, the everyday problems of dealing not only with one another but with children for whom you have ultimate responsibility for twenty-plus years. Yet it is those very married people who have in fact suffered and enjoyed that relationship who come to an outsider for advice. Having had the experience, they themselves don't seem to have been able to reflect on the experience and understand its implications. People come to a priest for advice not because he is an adept sexual practitioner but because supposedly the Church sent him off for a very long time to become wise.

In fact, one wonders if it isn't easier for a celibate to understand the problems of intimacy in a marriage better than a married person can understand the loneliness of celibacy. Giving up sex is the "easy" part. Far more difficult is never having someone with whom to share your soul totally, never having a child, battling to keep enthusiastic, fulfilled, and life-giving— without having sex. That same wealthy Jewish agnostic asked that same priest, "Honestly, do you mean to tell me you never have sex? Never?" And when the priest said he didn't, the man shook his head and said, "Then why are you happier than I am?" And he was.

As George McCauley writes, "It is at least arguable that the basis of people's trust in the priest stems in large part from his celibacy, which is a *sign of his commitment* to them.

One does not need to be black, or homosexual, or female, or male, or crippled, or sick, in order to empathize and understand, perhaps even more objectively. A psychiatrist needn't be mentally ill (one hopes), a cardiologist needn't have suffered his own heart attack. But in order to be a good confessor, one does need to have sinned.

Questions to Ponder and Discuss

✣ For many born Catholics, the sacraments are just a given, most often engaged in for reasons outside a person-to-Person "connection," like the obligatory visit to Grandma's or sending Christmas cards to people you don't truly care for because they'll surely send one to you. Since the Church and catechesis have turned away from the threat of hell and the overemphasis on sin that plagued the Church fifty years ago, the long lines for reconciliation have disappeared. Often when young people take a kind of "vacation" from involvement in the Church, they come back because they have some vague feeling that "It's good for the kids." But if the Church truly *is* the living Body of Christ, energized by his Spirit, then the channels of its lifeblood are the sacraments. In order for them to have a felt value, an individual seeking a closer involvement with the Church has to crave a meaning and purpose to life that just aren't answered in the less important operations of the week. If you've read this far, you must obviously feel that need. No matter how long or tedious the learning process, it *is* still worth it, isn't it? Ask yourself why. It really is important that you do, to grasp a motive that justifies going onward.

✣ As with any symbol, a sacrament is like the clothes that made the Invisible Man seeable. But in order to access the Presence *within* the sacrament, one has to have a different kind of receptivity than what one needs simply to apprehend the physical objects involved, like bread and wine, oil, incense, gestures, and movements. You can't just sit there, as you might at a film or a play, and expect the "actors" to do all the work. It takes a real *shift* from the ways we ordinarily apprehend and try to understand in our everyday lives. How can you sensitize yourself more to "enter into" the symbolic life of the Church? How do you cultivate that mind-set which penetrates the externals to the energizing Reality?

❧ Each of the sacraments is a rite of conversion, an experience which ought to change the way we handle our relationships. Do you genuinely *feel* a "connection" when you think of the Eucharist? Do you feel the challenge your baptism and confirmation have placed or will place on you as an important "agent" of the liberating Good News? Do you really feel as much responsibility as the clergy ought to feel for the apostolate of the Church? If not, can you understand what the obstacles are?

❧ Scripture: Matthew 26:26-30; Mark 16:15-16; James 5:13-16; Acts 8:14-17

❧ *Catechism:* 1066-1199, 1275-1284, 1315-1321, 1406-1419, 1485-1498, 1526-1532, 1590-1600, 1659-1666

This is the day the Lord has made.
Let us rejoice and be glad in it.

—Psalm 118:24

⁕ 14 ⁕

THE DAYS OF THE LORD

The Lord's Day. Sunday is "the Lord's day," when Easter returns every week and reminds us of the Good News that death has no power over us or those we love. Sunday is a call to reexperience what the two disciples underwent on the road to Emmaus that first Easter evening, when they thought all their hopes had been dashed. That story, in fact, is an outline of the Mass as it has been celebrated for two thousand years. They open their hearts to this stranger as they travel, and slowly he puts their problems into the perspective of the whole Hebrew Scriptures (the liturgy of the word). Then they stop for an evening meal and they "recognize him in the breaking of the bread" (the liturgy of the Eucharist). That is what the Sunday Mass is intended to do: put our lives into the perspective of the Scriptures and then join our Savior at a meal to celebrate the living presence of the Risen Lord in the midst of his own people. Liturgy is a time for *remembering*.

As Pope John Paul II wrote in his 1998 letter *Dies Domini* (DD—"The Day of the Lord"), "The resurrection of Jesus is the fundamental event upon which Christian faith rests" (2). As we saw before, if Christ is not risen from the dead, then all our faith is vain; the atheists are right; there is nothing after death, and all our struggles between now and then will finally be wiped out, purposeless, meaningless, absurd. Therefore, this expression of our faith is not just "part of the weekend," but a chance to *rejoice* at our own value, ratified by Christ's death and resurrection.

In the anthropomorphic description of God's six days of labor in *Genesis* calling forth the ordered universe, the earth and all living things from the primeval waters, culminating in the creation of human beings, on the seventh day God rested. "It would be banal to interpret God's 'rest' as a kind of divine 'inactivity.' It speaks, as it were, of God's lingering before the 'very good' work (Genesis 1:31) which his hand has wrought, in order to cast upon it *a gaze full of joyous delight*" (DD 11—emphasis original). It captures "the nuptial intensity which marks the relationship between God and his people" (DD 12). Therefore, our attitude toward Sunday and the weekly liturgy ought not to be something we merely endure, like an obligatory visit to a demanding old uncle, nor something to which we offer ourselves passively, but *engaging* our truest selves with the enlivening, liberating Spirit. Consider the meaning of "nuptial intensity."

The third commandment says: "Remember the Sabbath day in order to keep it holy" (Exodus 20:8). Time taken from the workweek for remembering *makes* the day blest. Resting therefore acquires a sacred value. The Jewish Shabbat is not only in imitation of the Creator who rested on the seventh day, but a time for them to remember that they were once slaves in Egypt and they are now free! We, too, are imprisoned in the weekly "rat race," but this is a time to put all our problems into perspective, as Jesus did for the Emmaus travelers, and comprehend our true selves: sons and daughters of the Most High! Peers of his Realm! It is not just an interruption of work but a *celebration* of who we really are!

Nor does this celebration stop at the church door. At the end of each Mass, we are *sent* to do what Jesus was sent to do: "bring good news to the poor . . . proclaim liberty to captives and recovery of sight to the blind, to set free the oppressed and announce that the time has come when the Lord will save his people" (Luke 4:18-19). Nor can we read Jesus' inaugural speech with only materialist eyes. There are souls in the week ahead of us that are poor, captives of greed and self-distaste and sexual drives, blind to the truth of their own value, yearning for someone at least to notice them, empathize with them, invite them. Who can reach out the hand of Christ to them?

The Small-C Church

Whether you worship in an enormous cathedral or in a rustic country chapel, the symbols are always the same—ornate or simple. Yet many born Catholics might be hard-pressed to explain their symbolism, having taken them for granted all their lives.

The focus of any church, of course, is the *altar*—as it has been since the times of primitive religions. It is the place of sacrifice and hallowed because of that. When the celebrant enters, his first act in the sanctuary is to reverence the altar by bowing and kissing it. In non-Catholic worship services which lessen Christ's presence in the Eucharist, the altar is similarly downplayed, in order to avoid what they believe to be idolatry of the altar, focusing rather on the service of the Word and the homily (sermon). In the early years of the Church, the Eucharist was offered in the catacombs, directly on top of a tomb of a Christian martyr. Today, altars contain a relic of some saint embedded in the center of the tabletop to remember that custom. Near the altar (but not on it) are candles. In the earliest churches, of course, they were needed for illumination. Today, they are a warming symbol of togetherness, as they are in any home at a special meal.

In a Catholic church, there is always a large *crucifix* with an image of the Body of Christ affixed to it, dead, as a symbol of the way to rebirth. Non-Catholic Christians have a bare cross, again avoiding the temptation to idolatry but more importantly stressing that Christ is no longer on the cross but risen. The Catholic symbol emphasizes that Christ is indeed still being crucified, in his members. Any other decorations are up to the tastes and proclivities (and finances) of the local parish and their pastor. But whether the sacred space is spartan and airy or dark and cluttered with all manner of icons, the place is still sacred, not because of its appearance but because of the One who joins us there and dwells there.

Someplace to the side or out of the central area is the *tabernacle* (the Latin word for "tent," which housed the Ark of the Covenant and the Ten Commandments), where the Eucharist is reserved at times when no liturgy is celebrated, principally for times when it is needed for *Viaticum* ("food for the journey," final communion for those in danger of death). But it is also there for those who find it helpful to their prayer to sit quietly and share a "connection" with Christ, physically present. Formerly, the tabernacle held a commanding space on the high altar, but liturgical scholars believed it intruded on the action of the liturgy itself. One of the most poignant symbols in any Catholic church is the *sanctuary lamp,* a flickering candle enclosed in a blood-colored glass, reminding the visitor that the aliveness of God is present in the tabernacle.

The *pascal candle* (Pasch, "Passover") a large wax candle blessed after the Easter fire is kindled during the Easter vigil Mass, symbolizes the light of Christ rising from death into glory. It is adorned with a cross, a Greek alpha and omega (beginning and end) and wax "nails." It is used to bless the baptismal font, plunged in and drawn forth (death and resurrection), and it remains lit during services for the fifty days between Easter and Pentecost, and at all funerals the casket is placed beneath it at the head of the center aisle—again, death and resurrection.

The *baptismal font* is a fixed pool or basin which is, very truly, the "vestibule" of the Church, the womb through which we all enter it. Some churches have a room set aside for the sacrament of reconciliation; others still maintain closeted *confessionals*. Most churches also usually have the *stations of the cross,* reminders of Jesus' journey from his condemnation to his burial. The road to the cross is the road to resurrection.

The *vestments* differentiate the ministers from the congregation. This doesn't pretend they are better than anyone else present but, during this time, the celebrant has been chosen to be a stand-in for the risen Christ, an instrument singled out to be used. The basic vestment is a white alb, a tunic like the earliest priests wore in Rome, worn by all the ministers of the Eucharist, even the altar servers. The priest and deacon wear stoles, lengths of cloth to signify ordination, the priest's hanging loose on either side of his neck, the deacon's over the left shoulder fastened on the right side. The priest also wears a chasuble, the outer garment of the late Roman world, colored in accordance with the season or the feast: white for the seasons of Christmas and Easter, feasts of Our Lord, Our Lady, and many of the saints; red on Palm Sunday of the Lord's Passion, Good Friday, Pentecost, and feasts of martyrs; violet for Advent and Lent; and rose for the "vacation" Sundays, Laetare and Gaudete, in the middle of Advent and Lent. The traditional symbolism of the chasuble is the charity that covers a multitude of sins.

The *vessels* used at Mass are quite simple: a paten, a gold-plated dish on which the large host rests throughout the Mass, a chalice, the cup which holds the consecrated wine, and often ciboria, large capped cups containing smaller hosts for distribution at communion. To emphasize the simplicity and to echo the original vessels used at the Last Supper, many churches use earthernware plates and cups.

Only two *books* are used in the Mass: the *Sacramentary* containing the prayers of each particular Mass and the ordinary prayers of each Mass, and the *Lectionary* containing the Scripture readings for each Mass, often carried held high by the lector in the opening procession.

The Order of the Liturgy. In his first *Apology* sent to Emperor Antoninus and the Senate, Saint Justin Martyr (d. 163) tried to explain just how the Church celebrated, showing that it in no way merited persecution.

> *On the day called Sunday there is a meeting in one place of those who live in cities or the country, and the memoirs of the apostles or the writing of the prophets are read as long as time permits. Then we all stand up together and offer prayers. And when we have finished the prayer, bread is brought, and wine and water, and the president similarly sends up prayers and thanksgivings to the best of his ability, and the congregation assents, saying the Amen; the distribution and reception of the consecrated elements by each one takes place and they are sent to the absent by the deacons. . . . We all hold this common gathering on Sunday, since it is the first day, on which God transforming darkness and matter made the universe, and Jesus Christ our Savior rose from the dead on the same day.*

In rough outline, that remains the order of the Mass today: the liturgy of the word and the liturgy of the Eucharist.

Introductory Rites. The ritual usually begins with the entrance hymn, sung by all the people to signify their unity, standing out of respect for the celebrant, the instrument of Christ at his gathering. The priest, servers, and liturgical ministers enter, usually processing from the rear of the church down the center aisle to bow to the altar and crucifix. The priest crosses up behind the altar, bows, and kisses it as a sign of veneration.

The whole ceremony begins with the sign of the cross, sealing everything with that unifying symbol of life through death. For a moment, the celebrant greets the people and often opens up the theme unifying the readings and the subject of the later homily. Then he invites them to admit in the quiet of their souls our common need for forgiveness before we begin the liturgy itself. After a moment of silence for each member of the assembly to ponder what that means personally, they communally recite a generalized confession of sinfulness (the confiteor), asking prayers not only of Our Lady and the whole court of heaven but of all those present. The priest then offers them absolution. Then, either singing or speaking, he asks for mercy of each of the members of the Trinity, and all the people join him.

After that penitential rite (except for the penitential seasons of Advent and Lent), the assembly recites or sings the Gloria, a hymn of praise and petition to the Lord Jesus Christ who takes away the sins of the world, the focus of all the Mass will celebrate. Next the priest invites the people to pray with him and pauses so they may do that privately before he reads the opening prayer or "collect" which gathers all their personal prayers into a common one, and the people respond "Amen" to it ("I agree" or "You speak for me, too.")

Then all sit to hear the readings for the day. Sometimes the readings are long, and one way to avoid the words smearing into one another is to engage the readings as if there were a chance one might be called upon to give the homily or commentary on them oneself, or to ponder what in the readings would puzzle the kids to ask about in the car on the way home.

The Liturgy of the Word. The readings are always centered on Christ, the first taken from the Hebrew Scriptures which point toward him, followed by a psalm connected to the theme of the readings, recited or sung back and forth between the reader or cantor and the congregation. The second reading usually comes from one of the epistles, followed in celebratory seasons like Christmas and Easter by an Alleluia. The Gospel is read by the celebrant or a deacon and we all stand, signifying the Gospel is what we "stand for." Then all sit for the homily, which ought to focus on the theme of the Mass and its pertinence to those assembled rather than on matters of parish business.

After that, the assembly stands for the Profession of Faith (the Creed), which again is what we stand for: belief in one God in three persons, Father, Son, and Spirit, in the incarnation of the Son, his birth by the Holy Spirit and the Virgin Mary, his death, resurrection, and return to glory, and our belief in the Church the Spirit enlivens: one, holy, catholic, and apostolic. And we conclude with our belief in the resurrection of the dead and the life of the world to come.

The liturgy of the word concludes with the prayer of the faithful or general intercessions, uniting to pray for the needs of our world and of our Church, uniting ourselves not only with the whole Body of Christ but to the world we are sent to devote ourselves to care for. To each petition the members respond, joining themselves to the prayers offered.

The Liturgy of the Eucharist. At this point, during a presentation song, some members of the congregation bring the vessels and the bread and wine down the aisle and hand them to the servers. In earlier times, the people actually brought farm goods, grain, and animals—as well as the bread and wine they themselves had made, as a physical sign of their contribution to the work of the Church and for the poor of the parish. Today, while the priest prepares the gifts, the ushers usually take up a collection for that purpose. (Which has its drawbacks, perhaps, but is a lot less messy!)

The celebrant spreads a corporal ("body cloth") on which the vessels will rest during the Mass, and lifts each of the offerings upward to God. He then washes his hands as a symbol of his desire for inner purification. Then the priest again asks the congregation to pause and pray silently, and then he gathers all our prayers into a single one, to which we respond, "Amen."

The preface is a prayer of thanksgiving. Although they change, they all basically testify to the same Christ-truths as the everyday preface: "With love we celebrate his death; with living faith we proclaim his resurrection; with unwavering hope we await his return in glory"—again and again the same truths: resurrection through death. It concludes with an acclamation of praise, the hymn the Scriptures picture the angels of heaven singing, unceasingly, "Holy, holy, holy, Lord God of Hosts, heaven and earth are full of your glory. Hosannah in the highest!" In a real sense, it is like the anthem played in civil cere-monies moments before the entrance of the Dignitary. In reverence, the assembly kneels for the actual consecration.

The priest begs the all-provident God to find the offerings worthy of divine acceptance and blessing, that it may become the Body and Blood of Jesus Christ. Then, no matter which canon the celebrant chooses, the climactic moment occurs when he repeats the words of Jesus at the Last Supper: "This is my Body . . . this is my Blood," ending with his plea that we make this same offering in his name till the end of time. He holds them up for all to see, then genuflects in reverence before the Timeless who has broken through the barriers of time and focused himself here in our midst. The people respond with one of the four acclamations which focus this action on the belief that, although Christ died, he is risen and will come again.

The ensuing prayers make it clear that the Eucharist is celebrated in union with the entire Church, both on earth and in heaven, and that the offering is made for all its members, living and dead, who have been called to share in the redemption wrought by Christ's Body and Blood. The consecration ends always with a declaration that all honor and glory are due to God the Father, through Christ, with Christ, and in Christ, in the unity of the Holy Spirit, forever and ever. To which the assembly wholeheartedly responds with the Great Amen, accepting that all that has transpired has the approval and acceptance of the whole People of God.

Then all those assembled say the Lord's Prayer, invoking the same Father we share with one another and with Jesus Christ. Acknowledging that, despite our differences, we are all brothers and sisters, we reach out and offer a sign of peace, uniting ourselves to one another as the Body of Christ before we are united with the very Body of Christ. Then the celebrant breaks up the consecrated bread as Jesus did at the Last Supper, dropping a portion of the bread into the chalice as a symbol of their unity, while the assembly petitions the Lamb of God for mercy and peace. Then he holds up the elements and says, "Look! This *is* the Lamb of God who takes away the sin of the world. Happy are we to be invited to his supper." And all respond with the prayer of the Roman soldier in the gospel that, although we are not worthy that he should enter our hearts, if he only says the word, we will become worthy of his presence.

While the priest and people receive, a communion song outwardly expresses our union in spirit and the joy that arises from our belief. After communion, there is time for all to reflect and commune inwardly with this enlivening Presence.

Afterward, the priest offers a final prayer which the people make their own with "Amen." He gives a final blessing and delegates us to take on the mission of Christ.

The Liturgical Year. The rhythm of the Church's year unfolds the whole mystery of Christ, from the incarnation and birth of Jesus, through his teaching and healing ministry, his passion, death, and resurrection, to his ascension and final glorification as Christ the King.

The year begins with the first Sunday of *Advent*, at the beginning of winter. The word "advent" means "approach." It is a reenacting, or at least an attempt to recapture the feeling of the centuries when the world did not know Christ, awaiting that liberation and fulfillment. Of course, like all reenactments, this expectation requires a certain "willing suspension of disbelief," since all of us know Christ *has* in fact entered our lives, that the Baby Jesus did in fact already come, and that he died and rose. It is at least remotely analogous to the realization suggested before about discovering how lucky we are but trying to imagine if we had never been given the gift of existence—so that we understand how precious existence (and all the gifts that arise from that) really is. (To capture that hope-in-bleakness and understand a world without Christ, read Samuel Beckett's existentialist play *Waiting for Godot*.)

Both Advent and Lent are times of penance, an invitation to spruce up the soul twice a year to welcome Christ into our lives. In the past, penance has always taken the form of self-denial, and there is surely a double-edged advantage, physical and spiritual, in gaining a firmer measure of control over our bad habits, whether it be in regard to eating, drinking, smoking, swearing, or whatever. There is one form of self-deprivation that would have benefits not only to oneself but to the needy: Develop a custom in the family of going through all the personal closets and bureaus and give away anything you haven't worn in a year. Obviously, you have no need of them, but they might keep someone else alive—or at least give them a thrill. Another positive custom might be, as a family, to make or repair toys to give to children who would have a bleak Christmas without them.

The gospels of Advent focus primarily on the preparatory work of John the Baptizer, a mission we ourselves share: Making straight the way of the Lord. In a perhaps crude analogy, John was the opening act who warms up the audience for the headliner. So too with ourselves. In a much less abrasive way from John's, we are sent to make the people we live and work with just a little less resistant to the call of Christ to richer lives.

Over the centuries, popular piety has sentimentalized the *Christmas* season into a kind of "Baby Jesus cult." It is true that there is a profound symbolism in the fact that, when the almighty and limitless God chose to become one of us, he came among us as the most helpless being there is: a newborn infant. But just as well-intentioned devotion has heaped up cathedrals on spots sacred in Christian belief—distancing us from them, so too Church art has swathed up the actors in the Christian drama in clothes they would never have dreamed of wearing—bringing out what was truly occurring in the spiritual dimension but also distancing the events and people from the ordinary kinds of lives we ourselves live. The gospels of the Christmas season, except for the fabulous arrival of the wise men, offer a much more homely picture: the birth of the Savior in a cowshed to a homeless couple, the Holy Family as refugees in Egypt, meditations on Mary the Mother of God, and Jesus' humble acceptance of a baptism of which he had no need. Even the Epiphany (Revelation), despite its elegant trappings of gold, frankincense, and myrrh (beloved of tasteful store windows selling luxuries rather than giving them away), tells a much more down-to-earth truth: Christ came not only for poor, illiterate, peasant Jews, but is equally accessible to wealthy, learned, high-born Gentiles as well.

Ordinary Time designates all the other Sundays of the year not clustered close to the two major feasts of Christmas and Easter. The first set occurs between the Epiphany and Lent, the second set between Pentecost and Advent. On these Days of the Lord, Christians continue to celebrate both the incarnation, God's entering our life, and the resurrection, our entering God's life. The gospels are a selection of readings centering at the outset on the beginning of Jesus' public ministry, his call of apostles, his preaching and healing, his conflicts with the Temple officials leading finally to their plans to trap him and do away with him.

Lent designates the forty gloomy days before the outbreak of Spring, in preparation for the remembrance of Christ's passion, death, and resurrection. According to the biblical tradition, the Hebrews wandered forty years in the wilderness preparing themselves to enter the new world of Canaan; Jesus prepared himself for forty days in the searing wilderness around Jericho to prepare himself for his mission. So we prepare by remembering.

Conversion is not a once-in-a-lifetime thing. Just as our ordinary physical lives are a series of conversions—from the womb to bodily independence, from infancy to toddling, from toddling to playing without an adult to mediate disputes, from the carefree life of the play years to schooling, from the ease of childhood to the challenges of adolescence, from an achieved sense of self to the adjustments of intimacy and partnership in marriage, from a tight union to the intrusion of children, through the advancing years to old age, so too with the lives of our souls. There is always a wider, deeper, richer life awaiting us—to which the two penitential seasons invite us.

Ash Wednesday is a graphic reminder of inevitable death, the one reality in our futures of which we can be absolutely certain. "Remember, you are dust, and into dust you shall return." Death is the crucial mystery. At that moment, we go on, or we simply cease being real. The resurrection is personally meaningless unless death is truly, personally meaningful. The readings of Lent ask us to remember Jesus' temptations in the desert and, in stark contrast, his radiant transfiguration, finally climaxing in what seemed his triumphant entry into Jerusalem on Palm (Passion) Sunday.

Even Jesus' closest companions did not understand his strange ideas on suffering and death as a necessary passage into a better life. *Holy Week* is a stark, paradoxical reminder that Jesus' death was not a defeat, but a victory.

It is interesting that, although nearly all the Catholic symbols so meaningful in my own boyhood have fallen into disuse, incapable of stirring a sense of "belonging" to the Church, the two physical symbols associated with Lent still have a felt meaning: the ashes of Ash Wednesday and the palms of Passion Sunday—which, ironically, are burned in order to produce those ashes. Yet again the paradox of death and triumph.

Holy Thursday celebrates the Last Supper and the institution of the sacrament of the Eucharist. At the central diocesan liturgy, the bishop gathers with most of the priests of the diocese to consecrate the chrism oil to be used for baptisms, confirmations, and ordinations, a Mass at which the priests renew their consecration to priestly service. In parish churches the rest of the faithful commemorate Jesus' two final commands before his arrest: that we should wash one another's feet and remember him in the Body and Blood of the Eucharist. At the end of this Mass the Blessed Sacrament, consecrated for the next day when there will be no Mass on the day Christ died, is taken in solemn procession to a place of reposition, and the altar is stripped of its coverings and the crosses covered— actions trying to recapture the desolation of those days.

Good Friday's liturgy has three parts. First, a reading of the complete passion account according to John, usually with various ministers and the entire assembly assuming parts. John's gospel stresses that Jesus was both the priest and the sacrificial lamb whose whole life was a "Yes" to the call of his Father. Therefore, his death on the cross was not a meaningless end to life but the culmination of a whole life of self-surrender. Breathing his last, he could say, "Now it is finished," and "Then he bowed his head and delivered over his spirit" (19:30) not only to his Father, but to us. The gospel reading segues into the general intercessions: for the Church, the pope, the clergy and laity, those preparing for baptism, the unity of all Christians, the Jewish people, those who do not believe in Christ, those who do not believe in God, those in public office, and those in special need—the sick, the dying, travelers, the imprisoned, the hungry.

Second, the veiled cross is carried to the altar. Part of it is unveiled and, one by one, all those present kiss it in veneration. After, the cross is placed on the altar, and the presanctified Eucharist is brought out for the third part of the liturgy, reception of communion.

Holy Saturday there is no liturgy during the day. The altar remains bare. A tomb.

However, in the early evening or at midnight in the early morning of Sunday, begins the feast of feasts, the celebration of our immortality in Christ. There are four parts: the light service, the liturgy of the word, the liturgy of baptism, and the liturgy of the Eucharist.

The vigil service focuses the symbolism of light and darkness. All lights in the church are extinguished. A fire is lighted outside the church doors, the priest blesses it and lights the Easter Candle from the new fire, saying: "May the light of Christ, rising in glory, dispel the darkness of our hearts and minds." Then the deacon (or priest) carries the candle in procession to the altar, singing, "Christ, our light," to which the assembly responds, "Thanks be to God." And in the complete darkness, smaller candles are lit from the larger one and passed to the people, each a separate light yet sharing it with their common source.

The liturgy of the word consists of readings from both

testaments interposed with psalms. Then children and adults are baptized in the usual rite, and the Mass concludes as always.

For the next five Sundays, the readings explore the appearances of the risen Jesus to Mary Magdalene, to the Twelve, to doubting Thomas, culminating in the feast of Jesus' ascension, then Pentecost, the Feast of the Holy Spirit, and the birthday of the missionary Church. The Sundays after Pentecost celebrate the Holy Trinity and the Body and Blood of Christ. Then Sundays of Ordinary Time continue to the celebration of Christ the King, and the whole cycle begins again with Advent.

These cycles gave a form and direction to the lives of the richest and poorest in European Christendom. It was much easier for them because they lived without our distractions. For them, their days were filled with the divine; for us, our days are filled with busyness and surfaces. That need not be. But achieving that sense of fulfillment-in-the-present takes effort, time, reflection.

Questions to Ponder and Discuss

❧ In order for the Good News of the resurrection to have any felt value, one has to have a very real awareness of death. It is inevitable, unpredictable, and—at least as far as this life is concerned—ultimate; it renders everything that happened before it unchangeable. But death has lost its bracing force in our society. On the one hand, it is hidden away in hospitals, nursing homes, and funeral parlors. On the other hand, death is trivialized by the media; any child has seen more deaths, real and scripted, than a Vietnam veteran, to the point they can't tell the difference. All of us have become hardened to horrific headlines. An overawareness of death can be crippling, yet a lack of awareness of it can be equally disabling. To check that denial of death: Consider the times in your life when a realization of death has been painfully inescapable. Meditate on those moments, and try to distill what death tells us about how to live. Then bring your attention to a crucifix and what that symbol means to a believer. What does someone miss by ignoring each liturgy's remembrance of Christ's passion and the weekly return of Easter?

❧ Mass was undoubtedly a more moving experience in the catacombs. List the reasons for that. Why are so many very old churches surrounded by the village's graveyard? In what ways could a modern Catholic develop the same profound sense of the Sunday liturgy's importance?

❧ We are hampered in our attempts to grapple with the supernatural realities of our lives by the elusiveness of symbols. On the one hand, they are our only way of dealing with and trying to "capture" realities we are sure are there—like love, hope, honor, the soul, the presence of God—yet on the other hand, making symbols carry and deliver meaning requires more personal effort than deciphering definitions and formulas. The symbols of our faith require the souls of poets, not the skills of geometers, logicians, and chemists. If our schools have left many of us impoverished of the skills of metaphor and symbol, where do we go to enliven them? (The whole Christian enterprise is about *enlivening*, you see.)

❧ *Catechism:* 1066-1209

There are moments when, no matter what the attitude of the body, the soul is on its knees.

—Victor Hugo, *Les Miserables*

≫ 15 ≪

PRAYING

No one reading this book does not feel the need for a deeper connection with God, which is what *religion* means, and participating in the liturgy is a true way to establish and support that connection. But at its deepest level, religion is a person-to-Person connection, not only with the communal support of one's fellow believers but one-on-one, alone with God. Weekly Mass is a good reminder, and most of us have the weekend off anyway. But taking time alone with God during the week, either to say prayers like the rosary or simply to sit quietly and receptive in God's presence, requires an active choice to carve out some time in the day which belongs to God. It's important, but there are so many other expectations, pressures, deadlines, that it takes a real act of the will to pull out of the hurly-burly at least for fifteen minutes to put things into perspective. Over and above that, many simply have never learned *how* to pray meaningfully alone, without a prayer book, just consciously being with God.

A good deal of the fault for that, I think, lies in our religious upbringing. Well-intentioned teachers believed it was vitally important we learn every Christian doctrine—from the manner in which the Trinity Family conducts its internal affairs all the way to the holy days of obligation. And there was an awful lot about sin in there—and guilt, punishment, hell, and damnation—to the point God was in danger of becoming a pawnbroker straight out of Charles Dickens. And they kept going over the same boring and irrelevant stuff: sacraments, morality, stories from the Old and New Testaments. But nobody seemed able (or willing) to spend the effort to help us *internalize* it, to see any pertinence in it to our everyday lives. They were more interested in conformity than conversion. So, without a personal relationship to the "Subject" of it all, it became as gratuitous and ultimately forgettable as factoring quadratics.

The people who try to make us literate Christians get so lost in explaining the signs that point to God—sacraments, Scripture, rules, history, church—they often forget to make us look in the direction all the signs are pointing. The God-signs become God-substitutes. The reason for this is that it's easier to teach rules and history and doctrines than it is to teach praying—just as it's easier to teach fractions and Latin grammar than to teach a love of logic and a sensitivity to nuanced language. We immerse ourselves in doable practicalities and lose the whole forest.

I trust the Trinity knew what they were doing on Sinai when they gave Moses those two tablets of the Law. Nice gimmick to focus the attention of an easily distracted crowd. But the audience was so wedded to the tangible and to numbers that it focused all its attention on those two stone lists of rules and forgot the light blazing from Moses' face, fresh from meeting God.

We don't know persons analytically. Yet God (so say the most analytical theology texts) is personal. But we treat him as little more than a character in a novel or history. As one senior said: "I treat God the way I treat all my parents' friends." To know God in any way other than the academic mode, we have to approach God as we approach any other person we want to know: person-to-Person. Till then, we're doing background research for a personal interview that never takes place.

Obstacles

The first obstacle to making praying part of our lives is making prayer seem worth the trouble, and the major part of this chapter will devote itself to showing how *not* praying is actually self-impoverishing. But there are other obstacles as well: fear of silence and solitude, finding the time, the impracticability of praying and its corollary: short-circuiting the calculating intelligence.

Silence and Solitude. Probably never in history has there been a society so addicted to distractions. Put any of us in an Iowa cornfield and you're risking mental meltdown. What did people do when they were walking to school before they invented the car radio, the Walkman, the pager, and the cell phone? All day long, it's busy-busy-busy, so that when we get home we just want to crash. After the dinner dishes are stowed away, any one of us is free to read a book, play Monopoly, build a cabinet, crochet a quilt. But how many of us really *are* free? Don't most people, with all the freedom of robots, gravitate to the couch and keep clicking the remote till we find the least unappealing show? Hour after hour?

There's something threatening about solitude today. Some tell me, if there's no one else at home, they turn on the TV, the stereo, *and* the radio! How do we get control over our addiction to distractions? The only things I can think of are conviction and resolution.

Finding Time. Finding time to pray depends, of course, on the importance one attaches to connecting with God. But those of us who will admit, however shamefacedly, "Of course praying is important but . . . ," hardly ever find a day when we can't find fifteen minutes to shower, shave or put on makeup, and dress our outer selves to face the day. (Nobody'll see the inner shambles.) All of us have some kind of "fat" during the day: riding to work, mind-numbing sitcoms, the phone, the hobbies, the golf game. Nothing wrong with them, only with their tyranny.

Impracticability. The only time praying is practical—thus remotely worth consideration—is when one is in need of a handout or some answers. "But God doesn't give me what I ask or solve my problems." Forgetting, of course, that "No" really is *an* answer, and that God's silence might be saying, "Look. What did I give *you* a brain for?"

Personally, I've pretty much given up on prayers of petition, since I said Mass every day for three years that my mother could die, and she didn't. Nothing wrong with petitions; the Best of Us prayed in Gethsemane for release from the torment ahead of him. The difference was that Jesus knew God wasn't going to answer his prayers. Like Our Lady at Cana, he was simply telling a Friend there was a need. When we pour out our sorrow to a friend at a wake, we aren't expecting the friend to bring back the dead. We draw strength to go on, from a friend who supports us by letting us know we're not alone. God doesn't play the game for us, just lets us know—if we allow it—that the game is played in a larger context than we're ordinarily aware of. And I sometimes wonder if, when we pray for answers, we spend so much time prattling along that God must say, "Look, I'll *try* to suggest a few things if you'll just be quiet and *listen!*"

The Analytical Intelligence. Akin to uprooting that need to dominate God is the difficulty of short-circuiting the discursive intelligence that is in full gear most of our day. We add budget figures, diagnose illnesses, follow recipes, try to figure out kids, keep to schedules—all day long, clickety-clackety-click. We've got to pull our selves off to the side of the road and find out where we're going—and why. We have to open the spirit within (which the analytical intelligence can't even comprehend), and allow the Spirit of God to invade our spirits, our souls, our selves. But that's difficult, again, because it means yielding center stage in our concerns to the One who has been center stage since before we even joined the cast.

Finally, there is the primary obstacle: What's in it for me? And that's a perfectly reasonable question. I think what's in prayer for us is that it will make us better human beings—better spouses, better parents, better servants, better bosses. And it will give us a perspective that goes far beyond the hurly-burly of the everyday and puts our problems into the world of God.

What's In It for Me: Humanizing

Many executives pay big bucks for courses in meditation, with no overtly religious concern at all. What they want is to focus themselves, get in touch with what is really important in their lives, see the garbage and reject it. There are many worthwhile effects from taking time to meditate which have no religious connection at all. Here are only five: simplification, perspective, freedom, feeding the soul, and wisdom.

Simplification. No one can deny life is too confusing. We live in the most complex time in history: Hurry, bustle, keep it moving, have it on my desk by yesterday. Every free moment, our senses are assaulted by billboards and ads and commercials shouting at us to buy this, buy that—or else! A hydra of conflicting expectations: peers, bosses, kids, meter maids, and muggers. Whose proposal got accepted, who's getting promoted, who's got a new Lexus. It's like being locked in an asylum for insane carnival pitchmen.

"Leave me *alone!*" Okay. Here's your chance.

Each of us, at the very depths, has a human need to become a hermit at least fifteen minutes a day. Not a hermit cocooned in the Walkman. A hermit. Without an eye of peace in the hurricane of our days, we're going to be swallowed up in the whirlwind.

Only for a few moments, detach yourself from everything that fluctuates and, at rest, let all the tension drain out: all the confusion, deadlines, questions. Merely *be* there: emptied, at peace, receptive. As Chesterton said, poets and contemplatives don't go mad; the "solvers" do. For a few moments, float easily on the infinite sea and enjoy the view.

Perspective. After seeing enough pictures of starving children in Kurdestan, Ethiopia, and Cambodia, at least the sensitive soul feels a twinge of guilt complaining that we've got tuna casserole and broccoli again. Similarly, pulling out of the hurly-burly for awhile shows us what's really important in our lives, in others' expectations, in all those shouting voices.

One day my friend, Ed Bartley, was grading *Macbeth* tests at his desk when his little daughter came up and said, "Daddy! Come quick! The birds!" But Ed was a man who got papers back the next day. With hardly a look, he said, "Not now, honey. Daddy's busy." He went on, unaware for a few moments that she was standing next to his desk, a fat tear running down her cheek. In that moment, he really saw her. She was more important than *Macbeth* and "promises to keep." Wisely, he let her lead him to the apartment window, and for ten minutes they looked at the birds on the roof. They weren't accomplishing anything, but something was happening. And three years later, Ed died.

Freedom. Many harbor a ludicrous idea that somewhere "out there," totally unfettered freedom is possible. But even Ghengis

Khan was *subject* to the law of gravity. He had to submit, humbly as a child, before storms and earthquakes. Whether he wanted to or not, he had to eat and sleep, have toothaches, grow weary. There was a limit to what he could drink before passing out. If he conquered all the world, he was still powerless as a peasant before death.

But most of the limitations on our freedom are *self*-imposed: enslavement to others' judgments, gigantification of our shortcomings, and at the root: fear. If we could just lay hold of our inner selves—beyond the power of others to warp that self-possession—we might find "the serenity to accept the things that can't be changed, the courage to change the things that can be changed, and the wisdom to know the difference."

True freedom comes from what Saint Ignatius Loyola called "detachment" or "indifference." Neither term implies that a person must become insensitive. The real meaning is "impartiality," that one seeks the freedom to do the truth, no matter what choosing the best option might cost. One chooses without possessiveness, without self-serving ambition, without impulsiveness, without greed, without vested interests. It counts the cost to the self later—if at all.

No one achieves real freedom until he or she can find what freedom truly means. And it doesn't mean living random lives.

Feeding the Soul. We're all smothered by reminders to build up our bodies—nutrition, workouts, rejecting drugs—which we hear with Buddhist attention. At least the young are also smothered with reminders to build up their minds—reading, learning to think by learning to write, getting those verbal and math scores up—which they hear with somewhat less attention. But there seem far fewer reminders that what differentiates us from animals is not our bodies or our brains—which they share— but our souls—which they do not.

The soul is the self: who I am; and starving the soul is self-impoverishing. When you look at me, you don't see *me;* you see only my body. You can make educated guesses from what I say and do as to what kind of self I am, but you don't see that self. The guards in Nazi extermination camps had bodies and brains, but the reason we can call them "bestial" is that they had lost their souls. When I honestly fall in love, it's not the yearnings of my flesh or the calculations of the brain that say, "Yep! This is the one!" It's my soul. When I stand in awe of a snow-capped peak at dawn or Michelangelo's *David* or a baby's fist around my finger, it's not my body or mind that says, "Gasp!" It's my soul. My intellect is intrigued; my soul is stirred. It's where all that's nebulous in me resides: honor, awe, loyalty, remorse, patriotism, a need for purpose and meaning, faith, hope, and love. Oh, the soul is there, all right.

The body gurgles for food, the mind itches for answers, and the spirit expresses its hunger in restlessness and discontent. So, if you're suffering from the Blahs or Nothing Makes Any Sense or One-Damn-Thing-After-Another, you likely suffer from soul malnutrition. The hungers of the body can be temporarily assuaged by cheese puffs and soft drink, the hungers of the mind by ball scores and gossip, and the hungers of the soul by fandom and soap operas. But the result of bad food and lack of exercise are the same for all three: flab. What you need is to exercise the one thing that separates us from beasts: the soul.

Wisdom. It's easy to differentiate between someone to whom you could bring your questions and someone to whom you could bring your pain. Someone wise does know which things cannot be changed and which can, and he or she is at peace with that. The wise person accepts things as they are, his or her position in the universe: far better than a rock or carrot or pig; far less than God. Science is not God, nor is progress, nor is money, nor, most certainly, am I.

Wisdom doesn't come from suffering. If it did, animals in experimental laboratories would be wiser than all of us. Wisdom comes from suffering *reflected* on, accepted, assimilated. But if one is so busy doing and experiencing that he or she has no time for quiet reflection, then life becomes not a connected whole but a pile of beads without a string. We have to take time to withdraw from the transitory in order to discover the permanent.

What's In It for Me: Divinizing

Becoming aware that one has been divinized by Jesus Christ, invited into the Trinity Family, is not the same as the self-aggrandizing divinization of Roman emperors. Rather, it is a felt realization of the numinous presence of God not only all around us but *within* us. God is there all the time, waiting, but, like God's forgiveness, God's will to share the divine aliveness with us can't activate until we invite it. It's the heart-stopping understanding that, despite our shortcomings, despite our seeming insignificance to most of those around us, the God who dwells in unapproachable light dwells within us.

On the one hand, relating personally to a God vaster than the universe takes a little doing. On the other, picturing God as the Ancient of Days on a throne both risks becoming an idol and flies in the face of what we know about reality, that God inhabits a dimension beyond the limits of time and space: God has no beard, no throne, no right hand, no genitals. Yet I still have to deal with God, person-to-Person.

Personally, I find a less unsatisfying answer in physics—or, rather, in *meta*physics, in "Einstein-plus."

Suppose there *were* a Reality faster than light; it would be everywhere at once, so superenergized that it would be at rest. And scientists now believe when they crack open the innermost kernel of the atom, it will be nonextended energy. Every object we see—though it appears rock-hard—is actually just another form of energy: e = mc². Couple this science with all we know from religion: encounters with God so often described as fiery bushes and pillars and tongues of flame. And realize that, when Moses asked Yahweh his name, the answer was: I am who am. God is the pool of energizing existence out of which everything draws its "is," "the living freshness deep-down things." It may not help everyone, but when I pray, I pray to a Person made of light.

"The world is charged with the grandeur of God." So are you. Bow to the divine in you.

Without real contact with the Person about whom the theology texts speak and whom the Mass celebrates, no wonder the texts are no more meaningful than the insights of a dead rabbi and the liturgy no more involving than a long lunch for a Guest of Honor who never shows up.

But the critical difference between praying and merely clearing the mind is the "connection": from the beginning of the praying and consistently through it, being explicitly aware that Someone else is there—silent, perhaps, but there, the God whose faithfulness, and forgiveness, and fondness for us are forever.

This sure looks to me worth finding time for.

A Different Way of Praying

After all the obstacles and alibis are overcome, there are a few requisites for praying as opposed to "saying prayers." Nothing wrong with that at all, but many people find this method (lifted pretty much from Zen masters) a better way of "connecting" to God.

First, you need a place where you're relatively sure you won't be disturbed—a room with the phone unplugged, a park bench, a chapel. Put your watch in your pocket or purse, loosen your tie, kick off your shoes. You're about to spend some time with an old Friend.

Second, you need a focus—a candle, a stone, a crucifix, something fixed to come back to when you're distracted—and you will be distracted, even if there's no one else around: Your belly gurgles; your spine cracks; "Oh, I've got to remember to call Harry." What I am going to suggest is a mantra, a word or formula recited over and over until the words fade away and the calculating intelligence is numbed. The rosary is a mantra. People say they don't say the rosary anymore because they can't keep focused on what the words *mean*. But that's its whole purpose! Most conversations aren't worth even remembering, much less recording, but there are actually two conversations going on—the surface level of the chit-chat words and the deeper conversation that says, "I enjoy being with you." That's what the mantra does: the content of the words fades away and you can concentrate on the real connection.

Another requisite is position. If you sprawl, you're going to fall asleep; on the other hand, not many of us can pretzel ourselves into a lotus position without long-term effects. Some like to kneel, but at least I find that, after a very short time, my focus isn't on God but on my kneecaps. Just sit, composed, expectant, and invite God's presence within you to make itself known, felt.

Finally, relax. Roll your head around your neck and imagine all the tensions and responsibilities draining down from your head into your shoulders, down your arms and back, down into your seat and your legs and into the floor. Focus on your breathing. Really *deep* breaths. In for five counts, hold, out for five counts. Concentrate on your breath; remember that in Latin, Greek, and Hebrew, the words for "breath" and "spirit" are the same words, the one gives life to your body, the other ignites your soul.

On the very long intake of breath, say the first half of the mantra, like "Jesus, Son of David," and on the long exhale, "have mercy on me, a sinner." Or "God, my Father . . . somehow you're alive, in me!" Over and over and over. Focus your inner attention not on the words but on the *connection*, on the other Person receptive to you as you are receptive to him. Just "be with" God, not asking anything, not telling God anything. Sit like a child on its father's lap.

And as my wise friend, Jack Scully, says, "You don't have to put a clock on it." Rest there as long as you're able, without a need to check your watch or make a deadline. For these few moments, the world can get along just fine without you—as it did for all those millennia before you appeared on the scene. And the world will be a lot better when you return from this time out of time. You will have better perspective, balance, peace, and the energy of the Source of it all.

Questions to Ponder and Discuss

❋ Saint Teresa of Avila, no mean practitioner of prayer, wrote: "Contemplative prayer in my opinion is nothing else than a close sharing between friends; it means taking time frequently to be alone with him who we know loves us." Asked about his prayer, a peasant told the Curé of Ars quite simply, "I look at him, and he looks at me."

❋ A very salutary exercise for anyone seeking serenity is to make a grid, seven days wide, and twenty-four hours tall. (It's simple on a computer.) Fill in all the inescapables: work, meals, Mass, study. It's amazing—and liberating—to find out how much real free time one *does* have. It's also beneficial to assess just how much of that free time is more or less wasted. Where are you going to slot in time to make a connection with God?

❋ There are other ways of praying, too. Theologian John Courtney Murray, S.J., said that even research is prayer, because it is a search for the truth, and there is only one Truth. When monks used to get so much joy out of praying that they curtailed their work to pray more, their abbots used to tell them *laborare est orare,* "to work is to pray." Baking, carpentry, plumbing, even lifting weights can be a prayer—as long as they're not done alone, as long as there is Someone working *with* you. When you're driving alone, put Christ in the passenger seat and just share the time and space with him. "If I went up to heaven, you would be there; if I lay down in the world of the dead, you would be there. If I flew away beyond the east or lived in the farthest place in the west, you would be there to lead me, you would be there to help me" (Psalm 139:7-10).

❧ Scripture: Matthew 5:7-13; 11:28-30; Luke 18:1-5; 22:39-46

❧ *Catechism:* 2697-2758